READER'S DIGEST

Fresh Fruit
& Desserts

Eat Well Live Well

Eat Well Live Well

READER'S DIGEST

Fresh Fruit
& Desserts

Reader's
Digest

Published by The Reader's Digest Association Limited
London • New York • Sydney • Montreal

FRESH FRUIT & DESSERTS is part of a series of cookery books called EAT WELL LIVE WELL and was created by Amazon Publishing Limited

Series Editor *Norma MacMillan*
Volume Editor *Norma MacMillan*
Art Director *Bobbie Colgate Stone*
Photographic Direction *Bobbie Colgate Stone, Ruth Prentice*
Designer *Giles Powell-Smith*
Nutritionists *Fiona Hunter BSc Hons (Nutri.), Dip. Dietetics, Jane Thomas BSc, M Med Sci, SRD*
Editorial Assistants *Zoe Lehmann, Anna Ward*
Proofreader *Alison Leach*

CONTRIBUTORS
Writers *Sara Buenfeld, Anne Gains, Carole Handslip, Beverly LeBlanc, Janette Marshall, Jenni Muir, Marlena Spieler*
Recipe Testers *Bridget Colvin, Anne Gains, Clare Lewis, Heather Owen, Maggie Pannell, Susanna Tee*
Recipe Testing Co-ordinator *Anne Gains*
Photographers *Sue Atkinson, Martin Brigdale, Gus Filgate, Graham Kirk*
Stylists *Sue Russell, Helen Trent*
Home Economists *Maxine Clark, Louise Pickford*

FOR READER'S DIGEST
Series Editor *Christine Noble*
Editorial Assistant *Caroline Boucher*
Production Controllers *Kathy Brown, Jane Holyer*

READER'S DIGEST GENERAL BOOKS
Editorial Director *Cortina Butler*
Art Director *Nick Clark*

ISBN 0 276 42421 2

First Edition Copyright © 1999
The Reader's Digest Association Limited
11 Westferry Circus, Canary Wharf, London E14 4HE

Copyright © 1999 Reader's Digest Association Far East Limited
Philippines copyright © 1999 Reader's Digest Association Far East Limited

Reprinted with amendments 2000

Notes for the reader
• Use all metric or all imperial measures when preparing a recipe, as the two sets of measurements are not exact equivalents.
• Recipes were tested using metric measures and conventional (not fan-assisted) ovens. Medium eggs were used, unless otherwise specified.
• Can sizes are approximate, as weights can vary slightly according to the manufacturer.
• Preparation and cooking times are only intended as a guide.

The nutritional information in this book is for reference only. The editors urge anyone with continuing medical problems or symptoms to consult a doctor.

Contents

Eating well to live well

Eating a healthy diet can help you look good, feel great and have lots of energy. Nutrition fads come and go, but the simple keys to eating well remain the same: enjoy a variety of food – no single food contains all the vitamins, minerals, fibre and other essential components you need for health and vitality – and get the balance right by looking at the proportions of the different foods you eat. Add some regular exercise too – at least 30 minutes a day, 3 times a week – and you'll be helping yourself to live well and make the most of your true potential.

Getting it into proportion

Current guidelines are that most people in the UK should eat more starchy foods, more fruit and vegetables, and less fat, meat products and sugary foods. It is almost impossible to give exact amounts that you should eat, as every single person's requirements vary, depending on size, age and the amount of energy expended during the day. However, the Health Education Authority has suggested an ideal balance of the different foods that provide us with energy (calories) and the nutrients needed for health. The number of daily portions of each of the food groups will vary from person to person – for example, an active teenager might need to eat up to 14 portions of starchy carbohydrates every day, whereas a sedentary adult would only require 6 or 7 portions – but the proportions of the food groups in relation to each other should ideally stay the same.

More detailed explanations of food groups and nutritional terms can be found on pages 156–158, together with brief guidelines on amounts which can be used in conjunction with the nutritional analyses of the recipes. A simple way to get the balance right, however, is to imagine a daily 'plate' divided into the different food groups. On the imaginary 'plate', starchy carbohydrates fill at least one-third of the space, thus constituting the main part of your meals. Fruit and vegetables fill the same amount of space. The remaining third of the 'plate' is divided mainly between protein foods and dairy foods, with just a little space allowed for foods containing fat and sugar. These are the proportions to aim for.

It isn't essential to eat the ideal proportions on the 'plate' at every meal, or even every day – balancing them over a week or two is just as good. The healthiest diet for you and your family is one that is generally balanced and sustainable in the long term.

Our daily plate

Starchy carbohydrate foods: eat 6–14 portions a day

At least 50% of the calories in a healthy diet should come from carbohydrates, and most of that from starchy foods – bread, potatoes and other starchy vegetables, pasta, rice and cereals. For most people in the UK this means doubling current intake. Starchy carbohydrates are the best foods for energy. They also provide protein and essential vitamins and minerals, particularly those from the B group. Eat a variety of starchy foods, choosing wholemeal or wholegrain types whenever possible, because the fibre they contain helps to prevent constipation, bowel disease, heart disease and other health problems.

What is a portion of starchy foods?

Some examples are: 3 tbsp breakfast cereal • 2 tbsp muesli • 1 slice of bread or toast • 1 bread roll, bap or bun • 1 small pitta bread, naan bread or chapatti • 3 crackers or crispbreads • 1 medium-sized potato • 1 medium-sized plantain or small sweet potato • 2 heaped tbsp boiled rice • 2 heaped tbsp boiled pasta.

Fruit and vegetables: eat at least 5 portions a day

Nutrition experts are unanimous that we would all benefit from eating more fruit and vegetables each day – a total of at least 400 g (14 oz) of fruit and vegetables (edible part) is the target. Fruit and vegetables provide vitamin C for immunity and healing, and other 'antioxidant' vitamins and minerals for protection against cardiovascular disease and cancer. They also offer several 'phytochemicals' that help protect against cancer, and B vitamins, especially folate, which is important for women planning a pregnancy, to prevent birth defects. All of these, plus other nutrients, work together to boost well-being.

Antioxidant nutrients (e.g. vitamins C and beta-carotene, which are mainly derived from fruit and vegetables) and vitamin E help to prevent harmful free radicals in the body initiating or accelerating cancer, heart disease, cataracts, arthritis, general ageing, sun damage to skin, and damage to sperm. Free radicals occur naturally as a by-product of normal cell function, but are also caused by pollutants such as tobacco smoke and over-exposure to sunlight.

What is a portion of fruit or vegetables?

Some examples are: 1 medium-sized portion of vegetables or salad • 1 medium-sized piece of fresh fruit • 6 tbsp (about 140 g/5 oz) stewed or canned fruit • 1 small glass (100 ml/3½ fl oz) fruit juice.

Dairy foods: eat 2–3 portions a day

Dairy foods, such as milk, cheese, yogurt and fromage frais, are the best source of calcium for strong bones and teeth, and important for the nervous system. They also provide some protein for growth and repair, vitamin B_{12}, and vitamin A for healthy eyes. They are particularly valuable foods for young children, who need full-fat versions at least up to age 2. Dairy foods are also especially important for adolescent girls to prevent the development of osteoporosis later in life, and for women throughout life generally.

To limit fat intake, wherever possible adults should choose lower-fat dairy foods, such as semi-skimmed milk and low-fat yogurt.

What is a portion of dairy foods?

Some examples are: 1 medium-sized glass (200 ml/7 fl oz) milk • 1 matchbox-sized piece (40 g/1½ oz) Cheddar cheese • 1 small pot of yogurt • 125 g (4½ oz) cottage cheese or fromage frais.

Protein foods: eat 2–4 portions a day

Lean meat, fish, eggs and vegetarian alternatives provide protein for growth and cell repair, as well as iron to prevent anaemia. Meat also provides B vitamins for healthy nerves and digestion, especially vitamin B_{12}, and zinc for growth and healthy bones and skin. Only moderate amounts of these protein-rich foods are required. An adult woman needs about 45 g of protein a day and an adult man 55 g, which constitutes about 11% of a day's calories. This is less than the current average intake. For optimum health, we need to eat some protein every day.

What is a portion of protein-rich food?

Some examples are: 3 medium-sized slices (50–70 g/scant 2–3 oz) beef, pork, ham, lamb, liver, kidney, chicken or oily fish • 115–140 g (4–5 oz) white fish (not fried in batter) • 3 fish fingers • 2 eggs (up to 4 a week) • 5 tbsp (200 g/7 oz) baked beans or other pulses or lentils • 2 tbsp (60 g/2¼ oz) nuts, peanut butter or other nut products.

Foods containing fat: 1–5 portions per day

Unlike fruit, vegetables and starchy carbohydrates, which can be eaten in abundance, fatty foods should not exceed 33% of the day's calories in a balanced diet, and only 10% of this should be from saturated fat. This quantity of fat may seem a lot, but it isn't – fat contains more than twice as many calories per gram as either carbohydrate or protein.

Overconsumption of fat is a major cause of weight and health problems. A healthy diet must contain a certain amount of fat to provide fat-soluble vitamins and essential fatty acids, needed for the development and function of the brain, eyes and nervous system, but we only need a small amount each day – just 25 g is required, which is much less than we consume in our Western diet. The current recommendations from the Department of Health are a maximum of 75 g fat (of this, 21.5 g saturated) for women each day and 99 g fat (28.5 g saturated) for men. The best sources of the essential fatty acids are natural fish oils and pure vegetable oils.

What is a portion of fatty foods?

Some examples are: 1 tsp butter or margarine • 2 tsp low-fat spread • 1 tsp cooking oil • 1 tbsp mayonnaise or vinaigrette (salad dressing) • 1 tbsp cream • 1 individual packet of crisps.

Foods containing sugar: 0–2 portions per day

Although many foods naturally contain sugars (e.g. fruit contains fructose, milk lactose), health experts recommend that we limit 'added' sugars. Added sugars, such as table sugar, provide only calories – they contain no vitamins, minerals or fibre to contribute to health, and it is not necessary to eat them at all. But, as the old adage goes, 'a little of what you fancy does you good' and sugar is no exception. Denial of foods, or using them as rewards or punishment, is not a healthy attitude to eating, and can lead to cravings, binges and yo-yo dieting. Sweet foods are a pleasurable part of a well-balanced diet, but added sugars should account for no more than 11% of the total daily carbohydrate intake.

In assessing how much sugar you consume, don't forget that it is a major ingredient of many processed and ready-prepared foods.

What is a portion of sugary foods?

Some examples are: 3 tsp sugar • 1 heaped tsp jam or honey • 2 biscuits • half a slice of cake • 1 doughnut • 1 Danish pastry • 1 small bar of chocolate • 1 small tube or bag of sweets.

Too salty

Salt (sodium chloride) is essential for a variety of body functions, but we tend to eat too much through consumption of salty processed foods, 'fast' foods and ready-prepared foods, and by adding salt in cooking and at the table. The end result can be rising blood pressure as we get older, which puts us at higher risk of heart disease and stroke. Eating more vegetables and fruit increases potassium intake, which can help to counteract the damaging effects of salt.

Alcohol in a healthy diet

In recent research, moderate drinking of alcohol has been linked with a reduced risk of heart disease and stroke among men and women over 45. However, because of other risks associated with alcohol, particularly in excess quantities, no doctor would recommend taking up drinking if you are teetotal. The healthiest pattern of drinking is to enjoy small amounts of alcohol with food, to have alcohol-free days and always to avoid getting drunk. A well-balanced diet is vital because nutrients from food (vitamins and minerals) are needed to detoxify the alcohol.

Water – the best choice

Drinking plenty of non-alcoholic liquid each day is an often overlooked part of a well-balanced diet. A minimum of 8 glasses (which is about 2 litres/3½ pints) is the ideal. If possible, these should not all be tea or coffee, as these are stimulants and diuretics, which cause the body to lose liquids, taking with them water-soluble vitamins. Water is the best choice. Other good choices are fruit or herb teas or tisanes, fruit juices – diluted with water, if preferred – or semi-skimmed milk (full-fat milk for very young children). Fizzy sugary or acidic drinks such as cola are more likely to damage tooth enamel than other drinks.

As a guide to the vitamin and mineral content of foods and recipes in the book, we have used the following terms and symbols, based on the percentage of the daily RNI provided by one serving for the average adult man or woman aged 19–49 years (see also pages 156–158):

✓✓✓	or excellent	at least 50% (half)
✓✓	or good	25–50% (one-quarter to one-half)
✓	or useful	10–25% (one-tenth to one-quarter)

Note that recipes contribute other nutrients, but the analyses only include those that provide at least 10% RNI per portion. Vitamins and minerals where deficiencies are rare are not included.

Ⓥ denotes that a recipe is suitable for vegetarians.

Super Fruit

Delicious nutrition for health and well-being

FRUIT IS PACKED WITH VITAL VITAMINS, minerals and essential fibre, all of which help to protect you against ill health and keep you feeling at your best. The more fruit you eat, the greater the benefits, and with so many kinds to choose from, there will always be something to tempt you. Fruit is an ideal basis for healthy desserts, as well as being an attractive addition to salads and many savoury dishes. And it is the ultimate convenience food, easy to carry and eat anywhere. This chapter gives an overview of why fruit is so good for you, what to look for when buying fruit, and how to make sure you get the most from its great taste and health benefits.

Fruit in a healthy diet

The wide variety of delicious fruit available today makes it easy to enjoy the many positive health benefits of meeting the 5-a-day fruit and vegetable challenge. All fruit is good for us, be it fresh, frozen, dried or canned, so whatever the season, there can always be something nutritious and tempting on offer.

Why eat fruit?

In nutrition terms, fruit is full of vitamins and minerals, in particular vitamin C and beta-carotene and the minerals potassium, magnesium and selenium, plus different types of fibre. All of these are essential for general vitality and health.

Eating more fruit also improves the chances of avoiding cancer – an increasing number of studies show that people who eat a lot of fruit and vegetables are at less risk of heart disease, stroke and cancer, particularly colon and stomach cancer and probably breast cancer. The exact components in fruit and vegetables that offer protection have yet to be identified, but antioxidant vitamins and minerals play an important role, possibly in conjunction with different types of fibre and other natural plant chemicals.

▼ Best fruit for bioflavonoids – citrus (skin and pulp), apricots, cherries, grapes, papaya, cantaloupe melon

▲ Best fruit for energy – plantains, bananas, fresh dates, dried fruit such as apples, figs and apricots

What fruit nutrients can do

• Antioxidants – vitamins C, E and beta-carotene and the minerals zinc, selenium, manganese and copper – have the ability to delay or prevent oxidation, the process that produces highly reactive and damaging free radicals. Free radical damage ages us and causes 'oxidative' changes that increase the risk of heart disease and cells that can initiate cancers. Vitamin E also protects against cancer and heart disease, premature ageing, cataracts and other diseases. It strengthens blood capillary walls and helps to generate new skin. Antioxidants also maintain normal cell function.

• Bioflavonoids are another type of antioxidant. They work with vitamin C to boost immunity and to strengthen blood capillaries, and act as anti-inflammatory agents.

Best fruit for fibre — bananas, oranges,
apples, dried fruit ▶
Best fruit for vitamin C — kiwi fruit, oranges,
strawberries, blackcurrants ▼

▲ Best fruit for beta-carotene —
cantaloupe melon, mango, peaches,
papaya, apricots
◀ Best fruit for minerals — bananas
(potassium), apricots, particularly dried
(iron), prunes (potassium and iron)

11

- B vitamins are vital for healthy nerves and releasing energy from food during digestion. Although in general fruit is not as good a source of B vitamins as, say, cereals, one of the B vitamins, folate (also referred to as folic acid), is found in oranges and other citrus fruit and in bananas.
- Fibre comes in several varieties, many of which are found in fruit. Soluble fibre (like the gummy pectin in fruit that makes jams gel) helps to lower levels of harmful blood cholesterol. Insoluble fibre, from the skin and fibrous structure of fruits, helps to prevent constipation and associated problems.
- Potassium works to balance sodium, thus helping to prevent high blood pressure. Most Western diets contain too little potassium and too much sodium, particularly in processed foods. Potassium-rich fruit like bananas and oranges are useful aids to getting the balance right.

Which are the best fruits to eat?

Eating a wide variety is more beneficial than focusing on any particular type of fruit because there is no proof that one single fruit is better than any other at protecting against specific diseases. To spread your intake across different types of fruit, regularly choose from yellow-orange fruit (mangoes, peaches, apricots, melon), citrus fruit, berry fruit (strawberries, raspberries, blackcurrants, blueberries), exotic fruit (guava, passion fruit, papaya, kiwi, dates) and others such as apples, pears, bananas, pineapple and plums.

Whenever possible choose fruit in season and eat it raw to maximise the vitamin and mineral intake – even quick cooking reduces nutrient content. Remember, though, that cooked, canned and frozen fruit are still quite high in nutrients – in fact, frozen fruit will contain more vitamins than tired 'fresh' fruit. Fruit canned in fruit juice has less sugar than that canned in syrup, and it has a more 'fruity' flavour.

Is organic fruit better?

Many people feel that fruit grown without artificial pesticides is the ideal option. However, not eating enough fruit and vegetables is more harmful to health than hazards from any possible pesticide residues. Government regulations are designed to minimise residues in fruit, which surveillance shows do not usually exceed Maximum Residue Levels.

The golden rule is that fruit should always be thoroughly washed, as this removes some of the surface pesticides, waxes and other treatments. If you plan to use the zest of citrus fruit, it is wisest to buy organic or unwaxed fruit because the waxes contain fungicide.

How can desserts be healthy?

Healthy desserts might sound a contradiction in terms. Yet puddings based on fruit can make a delicious nutritional contribution to a meal. Puddings need not be high in fat and sugar to be satisfyingly rich and sweet. A good example is bread pudding packed with dried fruit – this helps to meet the daily requirements for many nutrients.

Fruity bread pudding
A bread pudding will provide fruit, starchy carbohydrates (bread), protein (eggs) and dairy foods (milk). See Some more ideas, page 123, for the recipe

Eating lots of different fruit is the best way to take advantage of the vital nutrients each has to offer

▲ Yellow-orange fruit, such as peaches, nectarines and apricots, provide beta-carotene, as well as B vitamins and vitamins A and C

▲ Citrus fruits are packed with vitamin C and also provide fibre

Other fruits contribute gummy fibre (apples), energy (pears), potassium (bananas), vitamin C (pineapple), and vitamin E and the antioxidant beta-carotene (plums) ▼

Berries of all kinds give us vitamins C and E, plus fibre ▶

◀ Of the many and varied exotic fruits, fresh dates provide vitamin C, fibre and lots of energy, guava gives us vitamin C and fibre, passion fruit has vitamins A and C, papaya offers vitamins A and C and fibre, and kiwi fruit is loaded with vitamin C plus some potassium

A new look at favourite fruits

We tend to take for granted the common-or-garden fruit that we see every day in the supermarkets and greengrocers – apples and pears, bananas, citrus fruits, berries and melons. But their tremendous health potential demands that we look at them in a fresh light and make a point of eating them more often.

An ABC of common fruit

While we think of fruit as supplying mainly vitamin C, some fruit also contain small but useful amounts of beta-carotene, which the body can convert to vitamin A, plus the B vitamins, vitamin E, and minerals such as iron and zinc. All the fruits here are low in calories and fat free. A portion size is given to help you count your 5-a-day.

When buying and storing fruit, buy the freshest you can find, and buy it in fairly small quantities that you know you will use up quickly. The vitamin content, particularly vitamin C, will vary according to freshness.

Apple (1 medium-sized fruit)

It has long been said that 'an apple a day keeps the doctor away'. One study has shown that eating up to 3 apples a day for a month can help to lower blood cholesterol levels. This is probably because apples contain gummy fibre (pectin) and an antioxidant called quercetin. So now we might add to the adage '… and 2 apples a day keeps the specialist away!' In addition, eating apples can help to prevent gum disease.

◆ Choose firm, bright crisp apples. Store in the fridge for up to 2 weeks, and bring to room temperature before eating.

Apricot, peach and nectarine (3 apricots, 1 medium-sized peach or nectarine)

Apricots provide vitamins B_1 (thiamin), niacin and B_6, and are a useful source of the antioxidant beta-carotene. An average serving of 3 apricots also provides useful amounts of fibre and potassium as well as vitamin C. Peaches and nectarines share a similar health profile, with more vitamin C, less vitamin A and slightly less fibre than apricots. The darker the colour of the fruit, the higher the carotenoid content, so white-flesh peaches and nectarines will contain less beta-carotene.

◆ Choose firm plump fruit that yields slightly to the touch and has even-coloured skin. Do not buy fruit that is green near the stalk. It is unripe and will just go soft. Store in the fridge for up to a week, or ripen in a paper bag at room temperature.

Banana (1 medium-sized fruit)

Bananas contain high levels of natural sugars, and are a better source of energy than refined sugary foods because they have a lot more to offer. They are unusual amongst fruit because they are a useful source of vitamin B_6 and vitamin E, as well as providing folate. A medium-sized banana even contains a good amount of vitamin C, and the potassium content (10% RNI) helps to redress our typically high sodium intake, as well as replacing minerals lost through perspiration. Bananas really are a super fruit!

◆ If eating immediately, choose yellow fruit with a few brown specks; otherwise select fruit with green ends to ripen. Do not store in the fridge as this turns banana skins black. Instead, keep at room temperature, or in a cool place to slow ripening.

Berry fruit (1 cupful or approx 100 g/3½ oz)

The purple, dark red and blue colours that characterise many berries, such as blackcurrants, blackberries, loganberries, raspberries and strawberries (as well as dark cherries and black grapes), come from antioxidant anthocyanin flavonoids, which may help to strengthen walls of small blood vessels.

● Blackberries have similar nutrient levels to blackcurrants, but contain even more vitamin E – 2.4 mg per portion, making them the richest fruit source of vitamin E.

● Blackcurrants are outstandingly high in vitamin C, containing more than five times the RNI in a portion. In addition to vitamin C, blackcurrants also contain useful amounts of potassium, fibre and vitamin E.

apples

raspberries

bananas

nectarines, peaches
and apricots

blackcurrants
and blackberries

gooseberries

cranberries

strawberries

blueberries

- Blueberries contain antioxidants and nutrients similar to those found in cranberries.
- Cranberries are a good source of vitamin C and provide useful amounts of fibre. A regular intake of cranberry juice can be used to help treat or prevent urinary tract infections such as cystitis, because they contain a compound that prevents the most common bacteria which cause cystitis from becoming attached to the bladder wall.
- Gooseberries can be enjoyed during their short summer season as a good source of vitamin C and a useful source of soluble fibre.
- Raspberries contain half the vitamin C of strawberries.
- Strawberries are an excellent source of vitamin C, with a portion containing nearly twice the RNI for that vitamin – gram for gram they contain more vitamin C than oranges. They are also a useful source of folate.
◆ Choose firm, plump berries with a 'bloom' (e.g. blueberries and blackberries) or that are shiny (blackcurrants). Do not buy berries if there are white patches or any mould on them, or if damage to the packaging has caused juice to run out of the fruit. Use as soon as possible, storing in the fridge for no more than 1–2 days, unwashed and uncovered as they go mouldy quickly. When ready to use, rinse berries briefly in cold water and pat dry gently on kitchen paper.

Cherries (20 cherries or 80 g/scant 3 oz)
These are a useful source of vitamin C. In addition, they have a mild laxative action.
◆ Buy and store as berries.

Citrus fruit (1 medium-sized orange, ½ grapefruit, 20 kumquats)
All citrus fruit – oranges, grapefruit, lemons, limes, mandarins, satsumas, kumquats and so on – are very nutritious. They are an excellent source of vitamin C – one medium-to-large orange provides twice the RNI of vitamin C – and the membrane that encases each juicy segment is a common source of flavonoids and fibre. Pink grapefruit contains beta-carotene.
◆ Choose firm, well-shaped fruit that feel heavy for their size. Do not buy fruit with bruises or soft patches or that are shrivelled. Store in the fridge, or at room temperature. The thick skin helps to prevent citrus fruit from drying out.

Grapes (1 cupful or approx 100 g/3½ oz)
Deliciously sweet, grapes are a useful source of potassium and copper. Those with red and black skins have antioxidant properties as they are high in bioflavonoids (which is passed on to the wine made from the grapes).
◆ Choose plump fruit, either shiny or with a bloom. Do not buy if they are shrivelled, going brown or split. Store in the fridge for up to 4–5 days.

oranges, lemons, limes, kumquats

cantaloupe melon

cherries

grapes

pears   plums, greengages and damsons

rhubarb   watermelon

Melon (1 medium-sized wedge)

All melons provide vitamins B and C, although those with orange flesh, such as cantaloupe, contain more of these vitamins. The orange-fleshed melons also offer beta-carotene.

◆ Only some varieties are scented, so aroma is not necessarily an indication of ripeness, and melons do not have to be soft at the stalk end to be ripe. Do not buy if damaged or bruised. Store either in the fridge for up to 2 weeks (melons do not continue to ripen after picking) or at room temperature. Once cut, wrap and store in the fridge.

Pear (1 medium-sized fruit)

Although not nutritionally outstanding, pears make a great energy-boosting snack because they are slightly higher in calories than apples and many other fruits. Pears are one of the most easily digested fruits. It is rare to have an allergic reaction against them, so they are often included in exclusion diets used for identifying foods that cause allergies.

◆ Choose firm fruit that feels slightly soft and has a bright and even-coloured skin. Do not buy fruit with brown marks or soft spots. Store at room temperature for up to 2 days or, if ripe, keep in the fridge.

Plum, greengage and damson (2 large or 3 medium-sized fruit)

These contain useful amounts of fibre and beta-carotene, as well as vitamins C and E.

◆ Choose well-coloured fruit with unblemished skins. Do not buy soft fruit with brown patches or fruit with any hint of fermentation. Also avoid hard or shrivelled fruit. Store in the fridge for up to 2 days; use as soon as possible because plums go over-ripe quickly.

Rhubarb (6 tbsp stewed)

Although treated as a fruit in cooking, rhubarb is actually a vegetable. It is a good source of potassium.

Watermelon (1 medium-sized wedge or 200 g/7 oz)

Use this fruit as a nutritious and refreshing thirst-quencher – it contains over 90% water, plus some carotenoids, making it a useful source of vitamin A. Watermelon is also a good source of vitamin C (40% RNI).

◆ Buy and store as for melon.

The vitamin C–iron connection

Fruits such as oranges, strawberries and kiwi that are very rich in vitamin C have been shown to improve the body's uptake of iron from vegetable sources. This is especially useful for vegetarians and for the increasing number of people cutting down on red meat, which is the traditional source of this important mineral in the diet.

super fruit

Fruits from round the world

Tropical and exotic fruits make wonderful ingredients in fruit salads and sorbets, as well as adding exciting flavours to savoury dishes. They also offer additional nutritional benefits to our native fruit, so it's well worth getting to know them and how to enjoy them at their best.

An ABC of tropical fruit

Exotic and tropical fruits brighten our shops with their colours and shapes. Those featured here offer a potent combination of antioxidant minerals and vitamins A, C and E, which is often reflected in their vibrant colours.

Yellow and orange fruit, such as mango, papaya, persimmon, carambola or star fruit, and tamarillo, are particularly good sources of antioxidants such as beta-carotene and vitamin C. The fresh fruit contains more nutrients than canned and has firmer texture and bright colours.

For the fruit discussed here, an average portion is 1 cupful or 100 g (3½ oz) of the edible flesh.

Asian pear

Crunchy, juicy and slightly sweet, this type of pear is a useful source of vitamin C and provides some fibre. Also called nashi (the Japanese word for pear), Chinese pear and Oriental pear, it may be small and yellow-green in colour or large and brown, and the skin may be smooth or sprinkled with russeting, according to the particular variety. When cooked, Asian pears never become completely tender, but retain their shape and firm texture.

◆ Asian pears are hard when ripe, unlike common pears. Store them in the fridge, where they will keep well for a long period – longer than apples. They are delicious raw and chilled, as well as cooked.

Cactus pear or prickly pear

The fruit of several varieties of cactus, this has sweet, brightly coloured pulp that smells of watermelon, and a multitude of hard black seeds. The flesh is rich in fibre and also supplies vitamin C and potassium.

◆ Choose fruit that has a fresh colour and no mouldy spots. If it gives when gently pressed it is ripe (it should not feel soft and squishy). Fruit that is firm can be left to ripen at room temperature. Once it is ripe, store it in the fridge, where it will keep for up to a week.

Cape gooseberry

The juicy dense flesh of this fruit, also called physalis, provides vitamin C and fibre as well as beta-carotene. Sweet with a slightly sharp aftertaste, it adds an intriguing flavour to both sweet and savoury preparations, either raw or cooked.

◆ Choose yellow or orangy gooseberries, avoiding any that are greenish. If spread out, still in their papery husks, on an uncovered plate, cape gooseberries will keep in the fridge for up to a month.

Carambola or star fruit

This fruit is a useful source of vitamins A and C, plus potassium and fibre. Its juicy, crisp flesh and attractive shape make it a decorative addition to puddings as well as to savoury dishes, and it does not discolour once cut.

◆ Choose juicy-looking fruit with a good colour; avoid any with brown or shrivelled edges. If the fruit is at all green, leave it to ripen at room temperature until the skin is completely yellow; the fruit should have a lovely perfume when ripe. Once fully ripe, store the fruit in the fridge, where it will keep for up to 2 weeks.

carambola or star fruit

Asian pear

custard apple

cactus pear or
prickly pear

dates

cape
gooseberries

feijoa

fig

guava

Custard apple

Looking like a plump, yellowish-green pine cone, the custard apple, or cherimoya, has sweet, slightly granular flesh with large shiny seeds. It is a good source of fibre and also provides vitamin C and niacin.

◆ Choose fruit that is even in colour, with no dark or splotched areas. When ripe it will just give when gently pressed (like an avocado). To ripen, keep at room temperature; thereafter store in the fridge for up to 4 days.

Date

Fresh dates are energy dynamos – these little batteries contain 30 calories (kcal) per date. They also provide vitamin C (a 100 g/3½ oz portion, which is about 4 dates, supplies almost a third of the RNI) and useful amounts of fibre.

◆ Choose plump, glossy fruit and store it in the fridge, where it will keep for up to 2–3 days.

Feijoa

This elongated oval fruit has a thin green skin and slightly tart, softish granular flesh. An excellent source of vitamin C, it also provides small amounts of the B vitamins. Feijoa is delicious both raw and cooked.

◆ Choose fruit that is fragrant. If it is not tender, leave it at room temperature for a few days – eat only when ripe and creamy-soft, otherwise feijoa can be rather bitter.

Fig

Although not an outstanding source of any particular nutrient, figs have small, but not negligible, amounts of many vitamins and minerals and fibre.

◆ Figs bruise easily, so are best bought before fully ripe. When ready to eat, they will be soft and the skin will split.

Guava

A portion of fresh guava can contain over five times the RNI of vitamin C, and even canned guava contains four times the RNI. Guava is also a useful source of fibre. The hard, edible seeds are as high in vitamins as the sweet juicy flesh, so you may want to try eating them too.

◆ When tender-ripe, guava has an intense floral aroma. Fruit that is slightly green, but still tender with some aroma, will ripen at room temperature, so buy it if that is all that is available. Once fully ripe, it can be kept in the fridge for up to 2 days (do not refrigerate unripe guavas).

super fruit

19

Kiwi fruit

Just one kiwi fruit contains nearly the total RNI for vitamin C, so put aside your prejudices – caused probably by this fruit's overuse in restaurants when it first appeared here. It is also a useful source of potassium, and is low in calories, at about 29 kcal per fruit.

◆ When buying kiwi, choose firm fruit that yields only slightly when pressed. Avoid fruit that is damaged or soft, as it will be mushy and lack flavour. Kiwi continues to ripen after picking (it is picked while still hard), so keep it at room temperature and then, once ripe, store it in the fridge for up to 2 weeks.

Lychee

Eating 3–4 raw lychees will provide two-thirds of your daily RNI of vitamin C. As these fruit are so luscious and beautifully perfumed, this is much more pleasurable than swallowing a vitamin pill.

◆ Choose lychees that feel heavy and full, with no cracks or shrivelling of the shell. The rosier they look, the fresher they will be. The fruit, still in shells, keeps well in the fridge – up to 2 weeks, although some of the perfume will be lost.

Mango

The luscious mango, with its richly coloured flesh, is one of the best fruit sources of vitamin A (from beta-carotene), providing over half the daily needs in one portion, which is about half a large mango. It is also an excellent source of vitamin C, and provides useful amounts of copper and fibre.

◆ Green mangoes are not necessarily unripe as skin colour depends on the variety. For those varieties that become yellow or red when ripe, choose fruit that feels full, with taut skin and no soft spots. The fruit should have a pleasant perfume (sniff the stalk end) – the stronger the scent, the more ripe it is. Keep the fruit at room temperature until ripe, then use it without delay, as mangoes do not benefit from prolonged storage in the fridge.

Papaya

Also called pawpaw, this is another nutritious 'all rounder' with good antioxidant value – an excellent source of vitamin C, useful source of vitamin A and providing useful amounts of fibre. The softish seeds in the centre of the yellow or sunset-pink papaya flesh are edible.

pineapple

kiwi fruit

lychees   papaya

mango

passion fruit

rambutans

quince

super fruit

◆ Papaya is easily bruised, so it is usually harvested when very green and hard. It will continue to ripen after picking, although it will never have as rich a flavour as fruit ripened on the tree. Choose fruit whose skin has a good colour and no mouldy or bruised patches. Do not refrigerate unripe fruit; instead, let it ripen at room temperature.

Passion fruit

Although not nutritionally a champion, a passion fruit does contribute some vitamins A and C, and if you don't strain out the seeds it is a good source of fibre. Its major culinary contribution is its intense exotic fragrance. The granadilla is a close relative of passion fruit.

◆ Choose fruit that is large and heavy. Fruit with a dimpled skin is ready to use. If you can only find fruit with smooth skin, leave it at room temperature for a few days to wrinkle and ripen. Ripe fruit can be stored in the fridge for 1 week.

Persimmon

A good source of both vitamins C and A as well as fibre, the persimmon also provides some potassium. The variety most commonly available is the sharon fruit, which has flesh similar in texture to a firm plum.

persimmon
(sharon fruit)

◆ While some varieties of persimmon cannot be eaten until they are completely ripe and soft (otherwise they are mouth-puckeringly bitter), the sharon fruit can be enjoyed even when quite firm. Choose fruit with skin that is rich in colour. When ready to eat it will give to gentle pressure.

Pineapple

We are so used to pineapple that it hardly seems exotic, but it is certainly tropical in origin. Fresh pineapple is a good source of vitamin C.

◆ Choose pineapple with a fresh appearance, and avoid fruit with any soft bruised areas or leaves that are yellow or brown at the tips. A good indication of ripeness is a sweet aroma at the stalk end. Pineapple does not ripen after picking, although keeping it at room temperature for a few days will decrease the fruit's acidity and make it taste sweeter. A whole ripe pineapple can be stored in the fridge for up to 3 days.

pomegranate

Pomegranate

This is a fruit that offers good vitamin C and fibre content, plus a lot of visual appeal. The refreshingly acid-sweet pulp is a beautiful deep pink, looking like glistening jewels, with crunchy seeds inside.

◆ Choose fruit that is heavy for its size, with richly coloured, firm skin that has no blemishes. Pomegranate will keep well in the fridge for up to 3 months.

Quince

A portion of quince is a good source of vitamin C, although as this fruit requires cooking to be edible most of that vitamin is lost. Quince also provides a useful amount of fibre, and it is this fibre, or pectin, that makes quince so ideal for naturally jelled confections.

◆ Choose fruit that is aromatic. Once ripe (it will be yellow all over), it can be kept in the fridge, but wrap each fruit individually as quince bruises easily.

Rambutan

Called a 'hairy lychee' because its flesh is very like that of a lychee, the rambutan contains half the vitamin C of lychees.

◆ Choose fruit that feels heavy and full. If tender and ripe, store in the fridge.

Tamarillo

This egg-shaped fruit has a smooth, glossy, deep-red skin, and the dark apricot-coloured flesh inside resembles that of a tomato. In fact, its flavour is more like a pleasantly tart tomato than a sweet fruit – all of which explains why it is also called 'tree tomato'. A good source of vitamin C, this vitamin is retained if the fruit is used raw in a salad.

◆ Choose firm heavy fruit. When ripe it will give slightly when pressed and will be fragrant. Keep at room temperature until it ripens, then store in the fridge for up to a week.

tamarillo

Concentrated fruity goodness

Dried fruits prove the point that good things come in small packages. What they lack in size they gain in concentration of nutrients. And being small they make terrific snacks, especially for children.

dried Hunza apricots

An ABC of dried fruit

Drying food is a traditional method of preservation. Reducing the moisture content and concentrating sugars means bacteria cannot thrive. The result of drying fruit, whether in the sun or by industrial processes, is higher levels of carbohydrates weight-for-weight than fresh fruit. This makes dried fruit a great source of energy and an excellent snack food, particularly popular with small children. However, the high calorie content can spoil small appetites for meals and is also something weight watchers should be aware of. The high sugar content also means that dried fruit is best not eaten frequently between meals as this could increase the risk of tooth decay.

Many dried fruits are a significant source of potassium, and they contain useful amounts of minerals such as iron, as well as fibre. Drying reduces the water-soluble vitamin C content, but some B vitamins (also water-soluble) remain.

- Apples contain lots of fibre (40% RNI in just 100 g/3½ oz), plus a small amount of iron.
- Apricots are a useful source of vitamin A (13% RNI in 100 g/3½ oz), plus fibre. They are one of the richest fruit sources of iron, a mineral lacking in many women's diets and essential to prevent anaemia.
- Bananas when dried have five times the calories of fresh.
- Blueberries provide a useful amount of fibre in 30 g (1 oz).
- Cherries are lower in sugars than many other dried fruit. They contain one-third the fibre of raisins.
- Cranberries contain only a little less fibre than raisins and sultanas, and have many other good things to offer (see page 16). They are sweetened when dried.

- Currants provide fibre and magnesium.
- Dates are a very palatable source of fibre – they provide 10% RNI in just 4 dates. They also contain an impressive combination of nutrients, with small but significant amounts of the minerals potassium and copper, and the B vitamins niacin, B_6 and folate.
- Figs are best known for their fibre – in 2 dried figs there is 12% RNI. But they also contain an interesting mixture of nutrients: a surprising 14% RNI of calcium, a good amount of magnesium, significant iron (19% RNI for men, 11% for women) and potassium (11% RNI).
- Mango retains some of its antioxidant attractions and a useful amount of fibre.
- Papaya retains a lot of its brilliant colour when dried. It is a useful source of fibre at 14% RNI in a 30 g (1 oz) portion, and contains calcium.
- Peaches when dried contain twice the iron of fresh peaches (23% RNI for men, 14% for women in 30 g/1 oz), and they offer vitamin A and the B vitamin niacin. Dried peaches are also a useful source of fibre.
- Pears offer 29% RNI of fibre per 85 g (3 oz) serving, plus 18% RNI potassium and some iron.
- Pineapple tends to contain more additives than other dried fruit (e.g. acidity regulators, citric acid, malic acid, preservatives, sulphur dioxide). This may be because dried pineapple snacks are often made from the woody core rather than the main body of the fruit, which goes for canning.
- Prunes are very well known for their laxative role, with 3 prunes containing 10% RNI fibre. The same number of prunes also

dried strawberries

contains 10% RNI of iron for men and 6% for women, plus 7% RNI of potassium. In addition, prunes have an antioxidant role to play.

• Raisins and sultanas contain a useful amount of fibre. Their concentration of vitamins and minerals is lower than some dried fruit, but they are a useful source of potassium.

Sweet snacks

Most of the carbohydrate in dried fruit is in the form of sugars, but unlike refined sugar these foods are a valuable source of fibre and nutrients, making them a good snack food. They are also an excellent cooking ingredient – used with fresh fruit they can help reduce sugar or replace it.

Fruit and fibre – the GI factor

GI stands for Glycaemic Index, which is a ranking of foods based on their effect on blood sugar levels. Low-GI foods break down slowly, releasing energy gradually into the bloodstream, which results in a smaller rise of blood sugar. High-GI foods break down more quickly and cause a larger rise of blood sugar. Low-GI foods are more desirable because they can help to control hunger, appetite and weight, and lower raised blood fats. Fruit with a low GI include cherries, grapefruit, dried apricot, apple, banana, grapes, kiwi, mango, peach, pear and plum, and with intermediate GI cantaloupe, papaya, raisins and pineapple. Watermelon has a high GI.

Additives in dried fruit

Much dried fruit is treated with sulphur-based preservatives to prevent discoloration and to preserve and enhance the orange colour of fruits such as apricots and peaches. If dried fruits are unsulphured they are a less attractive brown colour and they do not have the sharp tang of sulphured fruit. Some people with asthma find sulphured foods trigger attacks. Potassium-based preservatives are used to prevent fungal and bacterial spoilage, particularly in ready-to-eat dried fruit that is partially hydrated for convenience. Fully dried fruit contains fewer additives. Dried fruit may also be coated with vegetable oil to make it glossy and prevent it from sticking and clumping.

Average calorie contents per 50 g (1¾ oz) of dried fruit

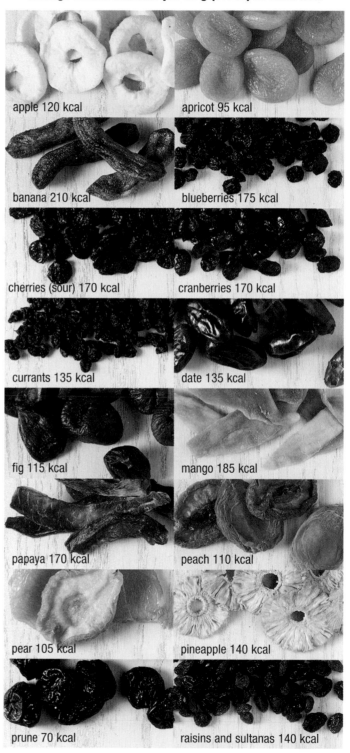

apple 120 kcal

apricot 95 kcal

banana 210 kcal

blueberries 175 kcal

cherries (sour) 170 kcal

cranberries 170 kcal

currants 135 kcal

date 135 kcal

fig 115 kcal

mango 185 kcal

papaya 170 kcal

peach 110 kcal

pear 105 kcal

pineapple 140 kcal

prune 70 kcal

raisins and sultanas 140 kcal

super fruit

Preparing and cooking fruit

After buying the freshest, best quality fruit you can find or afford, aim to use minimal preparation and cooking to retain the maximum vitamins and minerals. Serving fruit with a coulis adds more fruity goodness, and even the most reluctant child will enjoy dipping pieces of fruit into a small bowl of coulis.

Golden rules for preparing fruit
- Wash fruit well to remove surface dirt and bacteria. Some surface pesticides will also be removed by washing (special products do not remove much more than water). Rinse well in cold water, then drain or dry.
- Prepare as close to serving or cooking as possible.
- Avoid unnecessary peeling (vitamins and minerals are just below the skin, and the skin is a source of fibre).
- Do not chop too small.
- Dress cut surfaces with lemon juice to reduce nutrient loss.
- Cover and store prepared fruit in the fridge if not cooking or eating immediately.
- Never soak prepared fruit in water.

- Cook for the shortest time in the minimum amount of water, whether poaching fruit, boiling, stewing or microwaving. Steaming avoids contact with water, although some of the water-soluble vitamins will be lost.
- Avoid keeping fruit warm for long periods, or reheating it.

Saving vitamins and minerals
Vitamin A and its vegetable form beta-carotene are stable during mild heating, but losses occur at high temperatures. Vitamin E is destroyed gradually by heat, and the higher the temperature and the longer the cooking time, the greater the loss. Vitamin C leaches out during cooking because it is water-soluble. Minerals also leach into cooking water, but are not destroyed by normal cooking temperatures, so try to use the cooking water in the dish or include in syrups for fruit salad.

Good partners for fruit desserts

Cream on top – an occasional treat
Cream is a well-loved accompaniment for many fruit puddings as well as being used as an ingredient in both sweet and savoury dishes. You can enjoy cream as part of a healthy diet, eating a little occasionally and perhaps opting for creams that are lower in fat and calories. To help you choose, these are the fat contents and calories in different creams per level tablespoon: reduced-fat crème fraîche 2.25 g fat/28 kcal; single cream/soured cream 2.85 g fat/30 kcal; whipping cream 5.85 g fat/56 kcal; crème fraîche 6 g fat/58 kcal; double cream 7.2 g fat/67 kcal; clotted cream 9.45 g fat/88 kcal.

Yogurt – a better choice?
Yogurt is made by culturing milk with 'friendly' bacteria to thicken it. Plain yogurt makes an excellent alternative to cream, both as an accompaniment for fruit desserts and as an ingredient, but it's important to remember that yogurts contain differing amounts of fat and calories. To help you choose, these are the fat and calories for 1 level tablespoon of different yogurts: fat-free yogurt 0 g fat/7.5 kcal; low-fat plain yogurt 0.12 g fat/8 kcal; low-fat bio yogurt 0.12 g fat/10 kcal; whole milk plain yogurt 0.45 g fat/12 kcal; 'lite' Greek-style yogurt 0.75 g fat/12 kcal; Greek-style yogurt 1.35 g fat/17 kcal.

Frozen yogurt is a delicious lower-fat alternative to ice-cream. But it does contain a lot of sugar, and thus is high in calories.

The best of both
Whip a little whipping cream until stiff, then whip in the same amount of plain low-fat yogurt. Sweeten with a little honey or icing sugar and flavour with a few drops of pure vanilla extract, if liked.

Fruit coulis

Coulis are basically very simple fruit purées, made with raw or cooked fruit, sweetened if necessary. Coulis made with raw fruit will retain more of the vitamin C content, which is otherwise reduced through even the briefest cooking. Almost any soft fruit can be used for an uncooked coulis – kiwi, blackberries, peach, mango and papaya, to name just a few.

Berry coulis (uncooked)

Makes 200 ml (7 fl oz), to serve 4 with a dessert
125 g (4½ oz) raspberries
125 g (4½ oz) strawberries, sliced
1 tbsp fresh lemon juice or 1–2 tbsp kirsch
1 tbsp icing or caster sugar, or to taste

Preparation time: 10 minutes

1 In a bowl, mash the berries with a fork. Mix in the lemon juice and sugar. Alternatively, purée the fruit with the lemon juice and sugar in a food processor or blender.
2 Spoon the mixture into a fine nylon sieve placed over a bowl. Press the fruit through the sieve using a large spoon or spatula. Chill the coulis before serving.

Currant coulis (cooked)

Makes 200 ml (7 fl oz), to serve 4 with a dessert
125 g (4½ oz) redcurrants, stalks removed
125 g (4½ oz) blackcurrants, stalks removed
50 g (1¾ oz) sugar, or to taste
orange or lemon juice or crème de cassis (optional)

Preparation time: 15 minutes
Cooking time: 5 minutes

1 Place the fruit in a medium saucepan with the sugar. Cook over a low heat, stirring occasionally, until the sugar dissolves. The fruit should be soft with the juices running from it. Taste and add more sugar if necessary.
2 Press the fruit through a sieve as for the berry coulis. Taste and, if you like, sharpen the flavour with a little orange or lemon juice, or add crème de cassis for a sweeter flavour.

Some more ideas
● Gooseberries can be prepared in the same way. Use 250 g (9 oz) topped and tailed fruit and add 2 fresh elderberry flowerheads or 2 tbsp elderflower cordial and a little water to cook with the fruit. Serve with desserts or ice-cream. Or add less sugar and serve with cooked mackerel.
● For rhubarb coulis, use 250 g (9 oz) fruit, sweeten with sugar or honey and flavour with ground ginger.
● Make quick coulis with fruit canned in natural juice.
● Dried fruit (soaked to plump if needed), used alone or in combination with fresh fruit, make delicious coulis. Cook the dried fruit if necessary before puréeing.

Fresh mango and banana with berry coulis (above); Persian almond-milk jelly (right – see recipe, page 153) with currant coulis

A Great Start

Smoothies, muffins and other breakfast fare

ONE OF THE BEST WAYS to start the day is with nutritious, delicious fruit. Enjoy freshly juiced mixed citrus fruits, berries blended with yogurt to make a quick smoothie, or mango, peach and apricot in a fizzy drink. Sip a banana shake made with milk and frozen yogurt, or a refreshing icy pineapple and berry slush. Tempt your family with American-style apricot and nut muffins. Try morning toast topped with a spiced fruit spread, or a creamy mix of ricotta cheese, apples and dates. Or spoon up your own fruity muesli, or a crunchy cereal full of dried berries. Whichever appeals, fruit for breakfast will set you on the way to meeting the 5-a-day challenge.

Strawberry yogurt smoothie

This refreshing drink is perfect for summer when strawberries are plentiful and full of flavour and vitamins. It takes only a few minutes to prepare, so is ideal as a nourishing start to the day or as a light snack-in-a-glass at any time. You could also dilute it with more orange juice, to serve in place of sugary fruit squashes.

Serves 4

450 g (1 lb) ripe strawberries, hulled

grated zest and juice of 1 large orange

150 g (5½ oz) plain low-fat yogurt

1 tbsp caster sugar, or to taste (optional)

To decorate (optional)

4 small strawberries

4 small slices of orange

Preparation time: 5 minutes

Each serving provides

kcal 55, **protein** 3 g, **fat** 0.5 g (of which saturated fat 0.2 g), **carbohydrate** 11 g (of which sugars 11 g), **fibre** 1 g

✓✓✓ C

✓ folate, calcium

1 Tip the strawberries into a food processor or blender and add the grated orange zest, orange juice and yogurt. Blend to a smooth purée, scraping down the sides of the container once or twice. Taste the mixture and sweeten with the sugar, if necessary.

2 For a really smooth consistency, press through a nylon sieve to remove the strawberry pips, although this is not essential.

3 Pour into glasses. If you like, decorate with small strawberries and slices of orange, both split so they sit on the rim of the glass.

Some more ideas

• Add a sliced banana to the strawberries. This will thicken the texture of the smoothie and will also add natural sweetness, so be sure to taste before adding sugar – you may not need any.

• Swap the strawberries for dried apricots, to make a smoothie with a useful amount of beta-carotene and a good amount of soluble fibre. Gently simmer 200 g (7 oz) ready-to-eat dried apricots in 900 ml (1½ pints) strained Earl Grey tea for 30 minutes or until tender. Cool, then pour the apricots and liquid into a blender. Add the orange zest, juice and yogurt and blend until smooth. Taste and sweeten with sugar if required. Serve sprinkled with a little crunchy oat and pecan breakfast cereal or blueberry and cranberry granola (see page 46).

Plus points

• Strawberries are low in calories and are an excellent source of vitamin C.

• Most of the yogurt sold in the UK is 'live', which means that it contains high levels of beneficial live bacteria. Labelling does not always make it clear if yogurt is 'live', but if it is stored in the chiller cabinet of the supermarket you can be fairly confident that it is 'live' – that is, the yogurt has not been heat-treated after fermentation, a process that destroys the beneficial bacteria. The balance of bacteria in the gut is easily upset by stress, medication such as antibiotics, or a poor diet, but a regular intake of 'good' bacteria, such as that provided by 'live' yogurt, can help to maintain a healthy digestive tract.

Mango, peach and apricot fizz

A luscious combination of fruit puréed together with a little fizzy ginger ale, or with tonic, bitter lemon or sparkling mineral water, makes a wonderfully refreshing fruit drink with a difference – a simple way to boost your consumption of fresh fruit. Choose perfectly ripe, fragrant fruit for the smoothest fizz.

Serves 4

1 ripe mango
1 ripe peach
2 large ripe apricots
500 ml (17 fl oz) ginger ale
fresh mint or lemon balm leaves to decorate
   (optional)

Preparation time: 5–10 minutes

1 Peel the mango and cut the flesh away from the central stone. Roughly chop the flesh and put it into a blender or food processor. Alternatively, if you are using a hand blender, put the mango in a large tall jug.

2 Cover the peach and apricots with boiling water and leave for about 30 seconds, then drain and cool under cold running water. Slip off the skins. Roughly chop the flesh, discarding the stones, and add to the mango in the blender or food processor.

3 Pour over enough of the ginger ale just to cover the fruit, then process until completely smooth. Pour in the remaining ginger ale and process again.

4 Quickly pour into tall glasses, preferably over crushed ice. Decorate with fresh mint or lemon balm leaves, if you like. Serve immediately with wide straws or swizzle sticks.

Some more ideas

● Use low-calorie ginger ale to reduce the calorie content.

● So many different fruit and fizz combinations are possible. Using about 450 g (1 lb) fruit in total, try: raspberry, peach and melon with bitter lemon; strawberry, banana and orange segments with tonic water.

● When soft fruit are not in season, use fruit canned in juice as a substitute. A delicious combination is fresh melon, banana and canned apricots with sparkling mineral water.

Plus points

● These golden fruit provide a feast of vitamins. Peaches are full of vitamin C (100 g/3½ oz gives 77% of the RNI); apricots are a good source of the B vitamins (B_1, B_6 and niacin); and mangoes are an excellent source of vitamin A – just 100 g (3½ oz) of mango provides half the RNI of this vitamin, which is important for vision and for the prevention of heart disease and cancer.

Each serving provides Ⓥ
kcal 55, **protein** 1 g, **fat** 0 g, **carbohydrate** 14 g (of which sugars 13 g), **fibre** 2 g

✓✓✓ C

✓ A

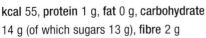

a great start

31

Banana and mango shake

A thick banana-flavoured milk shake with a tropical touch, this will certainly appeal to children and adults alike. Ideal at breakfast time as it is filling, nourishing and quick, it can also be enjoyed as a delectable dessert.

Serves 2

½ ripe mango

1 small ripe banana, sliced

150 ml (5 fl oz) semi-skimmed milk

120 ml (4 fl oz) orange juice

2 tsp lime juice

1 tsp caster sugar

2 heaped tbsp vanilla frozen yogurt

sprigs of fresh lemon balm to decorate
    (optional)

Preparation time: 5 minutes

1 Peel the skin from the mango and cut the flesh away from the stone. Chop the flesh roughly. Put into a blender with the banana.

2 Add the milk, orange juice, lime juice, sugar and frozen yogurt and blend on maximum speed for about 30 seconds or until mixed and frothy.

3 Pour into glasses and serve immediately, decorated with sprigs of lemon balm, if you like.

Some more ideas

● Use skimmed milk instead of semi-skimmed. Skimmed milk contains only 0.1% fat, as compared with 3.9% for full-cream milk and 1.6% for semi-skimmed milk, but still has similar levels of vitamins and minerals.

● Those who do not eat dairy products or who have a lactose (milk sugar) intolerance can substitute 300 ml (10 fl oz) soya milk for the cow's milk, and omit the frozen yogurt; or use 240 ml (8 fl oz) soya milk with 2 heaped tbsp soya ice-cream.

● Use a ripe peach instead of the mango half.

● For a shake rich in fibre, use 115 g (4 oz) stoned ready-to-eat prunes instead of the mango, with lemon juice instead of lime juice.

Plus points

● Milk is an excellent source of several important nutrients – protein, calcium and phosphorus (important for strong bones and teeth) and many of the B vitamins, particularly B_1, B_2, B_6 and B_{12}.

● Bananas are a useful source of the mineral potassium, a good intake of which may help to prevent high blood pressure.

● Mangoes are rich in carotenoid compounds and vitamin C, both antioxidants that protect the body against damage by free radicals.

Each serving provides Ⓥ

kcal 150, **protein** 5 g, **fat** 2 g (of which saturated fat 1 g), **carbohydrate** 30 g (of which sugars 29 g), **fibre** 1 g

✓✓✓ C

✓　　A, B_1, B_6, B_{12}, niacin, calcium, potassium

Citrus wake-up

What an invigorating drink this is, made with fresh citrus, very lightly sweetened and flavoured with a little lime zest and mint. Squeezing your own juice makes all the difference in both nutrition and flavour – even compared with buying 'freshly squeezed' juice – as vitamin C begins to dissipate as soon as a fruit or vegetable is cut. This mixed citrus drink makes a lively breakfast or brunch drink.

Serves 4

4 juicy oranges, about 500 g (1 lb 2 oz) in total

1 pink grapefruit

1 lemon

1 lime

grated zest of 1 lime

1 tbsp caster sugar

2 tbsp finely shredded fresh mint leaves

To decorate (optional)

slices of lime

slices of lemon

Preparation time: 15–20 minutes

1 Cut the oranges, grapefruit, lemon and lime in half crossways. Juice them using either an electric juicer or a simple citrus squeezer, preferably one that strains out the seeds but leaves in a generous quantity of pulp. If you have no squeezer at all, poke a fork into the flesh several times, then squeeze the juice from the fruit by hand, prodding with the fork now and again.

2 Combine the citrus juices in a jug with the lime zest, 4 tbsp water, the sugar and shreds of mint. Stir, then pour into glasses over a few ice cubes and, if you like, slices of lime and lemon.

Some more ideas

• Any juicy oranges can be used – shamouti Jaffa oranges are particularly delicious with their balance of sweet and tart. Or use tangerines, satsumas, clementines, mandarins or ortaniques.

• As a refreshing non-alcoholic alternative to wine or beer, dilute the mixture with sparkling mineral water – perfect for a sultry summer evening.

• For a Mexican-inspired citrus and mixed fruit 'zinger', omit the grapefruit and lime and use 2 lemons. Juice the citrus fruit and add the diced flesh of a ripe pineapple, 3 kiwi fruit and ½ cucumber. Serve either chunky, as is, for a sort of fruit gazpacho, or whiz it all up with a hand-held electric blender until it is frothy. Adjust the sweetening to taste (you may prefer no sugar at all) and decorate with fresh mint.

Plus points

• Citrus fruit are one of the best sources of vitamin C. They also contain compounds called coumarins which are believed to help to thin the blood, thus preventing stroke and heart attacks. In addition, studies have shown a correlation between a regular intake of vitamin C and the maintenance of intellectual function in elderly people.

Each serving provides Ⓥ

kcal 60, **protein** 1 g, **fat** 0 g, **carbohydrate** 14 g (of which sugars 14 g), **fibre** 2 g

✓✓✓ C

✓ B_1, folate

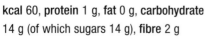

Frozen pineapple and berry slush

A cross between a breakfast sorbet and thick drink, this refreshing, virtually fat-free start to the day takes just seconds to whiz up. The secret of preparing it quickly is to keep a selection of chopped fruit in the freezer, then you can simply dip in to select a combination that suits your mood.

Serves 4

8 ice cubes

250 g (9 oz) hulled strawberries, frozen

250 g (9 oz) fresh pineapple chunks, frozen

120 ml (4 fl oz) pineapple juice

2 tbsp dried skimmed milk powder

1 tbsp vanilla sugar or caster sugar, or to taste

sprigs of fresh pineapple mint to decorate (optional)

Preparation time: 5–15 minutes, plus at least 1½ hours freezing of fruit

1 Put the ice cubes in a food processor or heavy-duty blender and process until they are finely crushed. Alternatively, crush the ice cubes in a freezerproof bag, bashing them with a rolling pin, and then put them in the processor or blender.

2 Add the strawberries, pineapple chunks, pineapple juice and skimmed milk powder and process again until blended but still with small pieces of fruit and ice visible.

3 Taste and sweeten with sugar if necessary. (The amount of sugar required will depend on the sweetness of the fruit.) Process briefly using the pulse button.

4 Spoon into tall glasses, decorate each with a sprig of pineapple mint, if you like, and serve with long spoons.

Some more ideas

• This is even quicker to make if you buy 500 g bags of frozen mixed fruit.

• Make a summer fruit slush with a 500 g bag of frozen mixed summer fruit, including blackberries, blueberries, cherries, redcurrants, raspberries and strawberries. Add 4 tbsp unsweetened orange juice and 2 tbsp skimmed milk powder and process. Sweeten with a little caster sugar to taste, if necessary.

• For a tropical slush use 400 g (14 oz) frozen chopped mango flesh and 1 fresh banana, about 100 g (3½ oz). Add 4 tbsp coconut milk and 4 tbsp unsweetened orange juice.

• If the recipe makes more than you need, freeze it in ice cube trays with dividers. On another morning, you can just whiz the cubes in a food processor or blender for an instant slush. Add fruit juice to dilute, if necessary.

Each serving provides Ⓥ

kcal 95, protein 3 g, fat 0.3 g, carbohydrate 22 g (of which sugars 22 g), fibre 2 g

✓✓✓ C

✓ B_1, B_2, folate, calcium

Plus points

• Fresh (and frozen) pineapple contains a substance called bromelain, a digestive enzyme that can break down proteins. There is some evidence to suggest that bromelain may help to break up blood clots and may therefore be helpful in protecting against heart disease. Bromelain also has an anti-inflammatory action and has been used in the treatment of arthritis.

• A wide variety of fruit is now available frozen. These are convenient to have on hand and may well be a better source of vitamins than some 'fresh' fruits that have been poorly stored or badly handled or languished too long on the shelf. They are particularly useful for blended drinks, where the texture of the fruit is not important.

• Dried skimmed milk powder, which gives this slush body, provides calcium, essential for healthy bones and teeth, as well as protein, zinc, and vitamins B_2 and B_{12}.

a great start

Apricot pecan muffins

Delicious American-style muffins are popular for breakfast and brunch, as well as for sweet snacks at any time. Packed with fresh fruit and nuts, and delicately spiced with cinnamon, the muffins here are lower in fat and sugar than bought muffins, and contain no trans fats or preservatives.

Makes 12 large muffins

250 g (9 oz) plain flour

85 g (3 oz) strong bread flour

2 tsp baking powder

pinch of salt

115 g (4 oz) light soft brown sugar

1 tsp ground cinnamon

3 tbsp wheat bran

½ tsp grated lemon zest

240 ml (8 fl oz) semi-skimmed milk

2 eggs

55 g (2 oz) unsalted butter, melted and cooled

225 g (8 oz) ripe but firm apricots, stoned and diced

55 g (2 oz) pecan nuts, chopped

Preparation time: 25 minutes

Cooking time: 20–25 minutes

1 Preheat the oven to 200°C (400°F, gas mark 6). Using a piece of crumpled kitchen paper and a small knob of butter, lightly grease a deep muffin tray – each cup should measure 6 cm (2½ in) across the top and be 2.5 cm (1 in) deep.

2 Sift the flours, baking powder, salt, sugar and cinnamon into a bowl. Stir in the wheat bran and lemon zest. Combine the milk, eggs and butter in a jug, mixing well. Pour into the dry ingredients and add the diced apricots and pecans. Stir just until the dry ingredients are moistened, leaving some small lumps of the flour mixture in the dough. Do not overmix.

3 Spoon into the prepared muffin tray, filling the cups two-thirds full. Bake for 20–25 minutes or until risen and golden brown and a wooden cocktail stick inserted into the centre of a muffin comes out clean. Leave to cool in the tins for 2–3 minutes, then turn out onto a wire rack to finish cooling. The muffins are best if served within a few hours of baking.

Each muffin provides Ⓥ

kcal 230, **protein** 6 g, **fat** 9 g (of which saturated fat 3 g), **carbohydrate** 34 g (of which sugars 13 g), **fibre** 2 g

✓ A, B₁, B₁₂, E, folate, niacin, calcium

Plus points

● Health experts regularly recommend that we should increase the amount of fibre in our diet. These muffins help to do just that, with fresh apricots providing a wide range of fibre components, including both soluble and insoluble fibre – not only good for digestion, but also helpful in controlling fat and sugar levels in the blood.

● Wheat bran contains the indigestible fibrous part of the wheat grain. It helps to provide the bulk that keeps the digestive system healthy.

Some more ideas

● For blueberry muffins, use 225 g (8 oz) fresh blueberries instead of the apricots. Substitute 1 tsp grated orange zest for the lemon zest and omit the pecan nuts.

● Chopped strawberries, peaches or nectarines can also be used, but the fruit must not be too ripe and mushy or it will make the muffin mixture too wet.

● Use 100 g (3½ oz) raisins or sultanas instead of apricots, with walnuts instead of pecans.

● To increase the fibre content, use 125 g (4½ oz) each plain white flour and plain wholemeal flour with the strong bread flour.

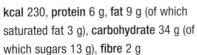
a great start

Orchard spread

Use this rich, slightly tart, lightly spiced purée of fresh and dried fruit to replace butter on warm morning toast or muffins. The recipe makes far more than 4 people can enjoy at one breakfast, but the spread keeps well in the fridge. Also try it with Cheddar cheese in a sandwich, or instead of pickle or chutney in a ploughman's lunch.

Makes 1 kg (2¼ lb)

500 g (1 lb 2 oz) cooking apples, such as
   Bramley's, peeled, cored and chopped
250 g (9 oz) ready-to-eat dried pears
250 g (9 oz) ready-to-eat dried peaches
360 ml (12 fl oz) apple juice
½ tsp ground mixed spice
1½ tsp lemon juice, or to taste (optional)

Preparation time: about 40 minutes, plus
   cooling

1 Place the apples, pears, peaches, apple juice, ground mixed spice and 120 ml (4 fl oz) water into a heavy-based saucepan. Set the pan over a high heat and bring the fruit mixture to the boil, stirring occasionally.

2 Reduce the heat to low and simmer, uncovered, for 30 minutes or until the mixture is reduced to a pulp and no liquid is visible on the surface. Stir frequently to prevent the mixture from sticking to the bottom of the pan.

3 Remove the pan from the heat and allow the mixture to cool slightly. Then taste and stir in the lemon juice if the mixture is too sweet.

4 Transfer the fruit mixture to a food processor or blender and process to a thick purée.

5 Leave to cool completely before serving. The spread can be kept, covered, in the fridge for up to 2 weeks.

Some more ideas

• Just before serving, stir in some finely chopped blanched almonds. (Do not keep the spread if adding almonds because the nuts will soften if stored for more than a few hours.)

• Make a spiced prune spread by replacing the dried pears and peaches with 500 g (1 lb 2 oz) prunes and using orange juice instead of apple juice. Omit the mixed spice and instead add the seeds from 3 crushed green cardamom pods.

• For a vanilla peach spread, replace the dried pears with additional dried peaches and use orange juice instead of apple juice. Omit the mixed spice and include a vanilla pod in the mixture while it simmers.

• Other combinations to try include apples and dried cranberries flavoured with finely grated orange zest, and apples and prunes flavoured with ground ginger and very finely diced pieces of stem ginger.

A 30 g (1 oz) serving provides Ⓥ
kcal 40, protein 0.5 g, fat 0.1 g,
carbohydrate 10 g (of which sugars 10 g),
fibre 1 g

✓   C

Plus points

• Apples are a good source of soluble fibre (pectin), and they provide vitamin C.
• Dried peaches are a good source of potassium. They also provide useful amounts of iron, carotenes and the B vitamin niacin.
• Both dried peaches and dried pears are good sources of fibre.
• The sweetness of fresh fruit is concentrated in their dried forms, so spreads such as this need no additional sugar to make them as sweet as commercial jams and preserves.

Spicy date, apple and ricotta dip

The natural sweetness of dates makes them an excellent sweetener in desserts, cakes and chutneys. Here they are cooked until smooth and pulpy with apple and aromatic spices to create a dip to serve with fruit and vegetable pieces. Alternatively, use this as an unusual topping for toast, scones or sweet crostini made with fruited bread.

Serves 4

3 green cardamom pods

1 Bramley's cooking apple, about 225 g (8 oz), peeled and roughly chopped

125 g (4½ oz) stoned dried dates, roughly chopped

½ tsp ground cinnamon

250 g (9 oz) ricotta cheese

To serve

crudités such as wedges of red and green-skinned apples, carrot, celery and cucumber sticks, wedges of pineapple, seedless grapes and slices of carambola

Preparation time: 15–20 minutes, plus cooling

1 Lightly crush the cardamom pods with the flat side of a chef's knife to split them open, then remove the seeds. Discard the pods and crush the seeds with the side of the knife. (This can be done with a pestle and mortar.)

2 Put the apple, dates, crushed cardamom seeds and cinnamon in a saucepan with 200 ml (7 fl oz) water. Bring to the boil over a moderate heat, stirring occasionally. Turn down the heat and simmer for 10 minutes or until the apples are cooked and the dates are pulpy. Stir the mixture occasionally during cooking.

3 Remove from the heat and leave to cool. When the apple mixture is cold, beat in the ricotta cheese. Keep, covered, in the fridge until needed. (The dip will keep for 3–4 days.)

4 Serve in a shallow bowl or dish surrounded by an assortment of fruit and vegetable crudités.

Plus points

● Ricotta is an Italian cheese made from the whey drained off when making cheeses such as mozzarella. It has a high moisture content, which makes it lower in fat and calories than many other soft, creamy cheeses.

● In common with all cheeses, ricotta is a good source of calcium, and it contains vitamins A and D. Less of these vitamins are present in low-fat cheeses such as ricotta – vitamin D is fat-soluble, so the less fat in the cheese, the less vitamin D – but the amounts are still useful

● The apple and dried dates provide useful amounts of fibre.

● Both cinnamon and cardamom are spices that can help to relieve indigestion. Also, cinnamon acts as a nasal decongestant.

Some more ideas

● To make a date, apple and orange dip, omit the ricotta cheese and instead beat in the grated zest and juice of 1 large orange. Pile into a bowl and serve surrounded with chunky wedges of apple and pear, and sticks of celery and carrot.

● Use as a cake or pancake filling.

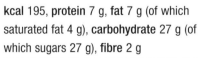

Each serving (dip alone) provides Ⓥ

kcal 195, **protein** 7 g, **fat** 7 g (of which saturated fat 4 g), **carbohydrate** 27 g (of which sugars 27 g), **fibre** 2 g

✓   A, B₁₂, C, niacin, calcium

a great start

Fresh fruit muesli

Fresh muesli, moist from soaking and rich with juicy fruit, is a revelation to those who have only eaten dried muesli. It has the soft consistency of porridge but the freshness of raw ingredients. This one is chock-full of both dried and ripe fresh fruit, making it a very satisfying way to start the day.

Serves 6

85 g (3 oz) bulghur wheat

115 g (4 oz) porridge oats

240 ml (8 fl oz) apple juice

50 g (1¾ oz) slivered unblanched almonds

3 tbsp pine nuts

2 tbsp shelled raw sunflower seeds

10 ready-to-eat dried apricots, diced

10 ready-to-eat dried figs, stalks removed, then diced

3 tbsp light soft brown sugar

2 green-skinned dessert apples, cored and coarsely grated

1 large or 2 small sharon fruit (persimmon), peeled and diced

1 passion fruit

few drops of pure almond extract (optional)

To decorate

pomegranate seeds or blueberries

extra diced sharon fruit (persimmon)

Preparation time: 15 minutes, plus 30 minutes soaking

Each serving provides Ⓥ

kcal 375, **protein** 9 g, **fat** 13 g (of which saturated fat 1 g), **carbohydrate** 56 g (of which sugars 33 g), **fibre** 6 g

✓✓✓	E
✓✓	B₁, C, iron
✓	B₂, folate, niacin, calcium, potassium, zinc

1 In a large bowl, combine the bulghur wheat with 240 ml (8 fl oz) water and stir to combine. Cover and leave to soak for 30 minutes to soften the bulghur. Drain well in a sieve and return to the bowl.

2 Add the porridge oats, apple juice, almonds, pine nuts, sunflower seeds, apricots, figs, brown sugar, grated apple and diced sharon fruit. Fold into the bulghur wheat.

3 Cut the passion fruit in half. Place a sieve over the bowl of muesli and spoon the passion fruit pulp and seeds into it. Press until the juice has gone through the sieve and only the seeds are left behind. Discard the seeds.

4 Add the almond extract, if using, and a little more apple juice if needed to make a moist but not sloppy consistency. Keep, covered, in the fridge until ready to eat, then serve topped with pomegranate seeds or blueberries, whichever is in season, plus additional sharon fruit. The muesli can be kept in the fridge, tightly covered, for up to 2 days. Stir it well before serving, and then add the fresh fruit decoration.

Some more ideas

● This makes a wonderful breakfast for those who do not eat dairy products. If you do eat dairy products, consider serving a large spoonful of plain yogurt on top of your muesli or perhaps layering it with yogurt, like a sundae.

● Use nectarines or firm pears instead of sharon fruit.

● Substitute a handful of dried cherries for the dried apricots.

● Use pear juice or white grape juice instead of apple juice.

● Decorate each serving with fresh cherries instead of pomegranate seeds or blueberries.

Plus points

● Porridge oats are an excellent source of soluble fibre which can help to reduce high blood cholesterol levels.

● Sunflower seeds are a rich source of vitamin E, an antioxidant that helps to protect cell membranes from damage by free radicals (thus helping to protect against heart disease and cancer). They also provide useful amounts of the B vitamins B₁ and niacin, and the mineral zinc.

● Dried figs are a good source of potassium, calcium and iron as well as fibre, both soluble and insoluble (which helps to prevent constipation).

Blueberry and cranberry granola

A delicious toasted muesli, this is made from a tempting mix of grains, nuts, seeds and colourful red and blue berries. Stirring maple syrup and orange juice into the mix helps to keep the oil content down, making this version much lower in fat than most ready-made 'crunchy' cereals.

Makes 500 g (1 lb 2 oz)

225 g (8 oz) rolled oats

45 g (1½ oz) wheatgerm

55 g (2 oz) millet flakes

1 tbsp sesame seeds

2 tbsp sunflower seeds

2 tbsp slivered almonds

50 g (1¾ oz) dried blueberries

50 g (1¾ oz) dried cranberries

15 g (½ oz) soft brown or demerara sugar

2 tbsp maple syrup

2 tbsp sunflower oil

2 tbsp orange juice

Preparation time: 40–50 minutes, plus cooling

1 Preheat the oven to 160°C (325°F, gas mark 3). In a large bowl, combine the oats, wheatgerm, millet flakes, sesame and sunflower seeds, almonds, dried berries and sugar. Stir until well mixed.

2 Put the maple syrup, oil and orange juice in a small jug and whisk together. Pour this mixture slowly into the dry ingredients, stirring to ensure that the liquid is evenly distributed and coats everything lightly.

3 Spread the mixture out evenly in a non-stick roasting tin. Bake for 30–40 minutes or until slightly crisp and lightly browned. Stir the mixture every 10 minutes to encourage even browning.

4 Remove from the oven and leave to cool. Store in an airtight container for up to 2 weeks. Serve with yogurt, milk or fruit juice.

Plus points

• This is a delicious way to get plenty of fibre, B vitamins and essential fatty acids. Wheatgerm is especially rich in B vitamins.

• A special feature of this recipe is the use of sunflower seeds, which not only add flavour but are also a rich source of nutrients. They are rich in healthy, polyunsaturated fat, and also provide plenty of magnesium, copper, iron and several B vitamins. Both sesame seeds and sunflower seeds can provide useful amounts of calcium, which is particularly important for people who do not include milk or cheese in their diet.

Some more ideas

• For a chunkier granola, replace the millet with barley flakes and the berries with a mixture of roughly chopped dried apples or apricots, prunes and dates. A little shredded coconut can also be added, if liked.

• The maple syrup can be replaced with clear honey, and the slivered almonds with chopped hazelnuts.

• If you prefer, use all dried blueberries or cranberries, or replace some or all of the berries with dried cherries.

A 60 g (2¼ oz) serving provides Ⓥ

kcal 250, **protein** 7 g, **fat** 11 g (of which saturated fat 0.8 g), **carbohydrate** 32 g (of which sugars 7 g), **fibre** 4 g

✓✓✓	E
✓✓	B₁
✓	B₂, B₆, folate, niacin

Raw Vitality

Fruit and vegetable salads, full of vitamin C

EATING FRESH FRUIT RAW lets you take maximum advantage of the wonderful nutrients on offer – particularly vitamin C. Salads, both sweet and savoury, are a superb way to enjoy fresh fruit. You can make a simple yet stunning spring or summer fruit salad with seasonal mixed berries, or with a combination of fresh and canned fruit such as lychees at any time of the year. The sweetness of luscious, ripe fruit contrasts beautifully with savoury ingredients in starters or main dish salads – try it with tender young vegetables such as peppers, cauliflower and celery, with Parma ham, crunchy nuts and seeds, and delicious cheeses of all kinds.

Berry salad with passion fruit

Berries are the utterly fresh flavour of summer. Tart, sweet and juicy, they come in a wide array of types, ranging from bright and delicate raspberries to fleshy strawberries, plump little blueberries and rich blackberries. The passion fruit is not a distinctive flavour in this dish, but instead it adds a fragrant tart edge.

Serves 6

450 g (1 lb) strawberries, cut in half

150 g (5½ oz) raspberries

100 g (3½ oz) blackberries

100 g (3½ oz) blueberries

100 g (3½ oz) mixed redcurrants and
blackcurrants, removed from their stalks

2 passion fruit

1 tbsp caster sugar

juice of ½ lemon or lime

Preparation time: 10–15 minutes

1 Mix the strawberries, raspberries, blackberries, blueberries, redcurrants and blackcurrants together in a bowl.

2 Cut the passion fruit in half. Holding a sieve over the bowl of berries, spoon the passion fruit flesh and seeds into the sieve. Rub the flesh and seeds briskly to press all the juice through the sieve onto the berries. Reserve a few of the passion fruit seeds left in the sieve and discard the rest.

3 Add the sugar and lemon or lime juice to the berries. Gently toss together. Sprinkle over the reserved passion fruit seeds. Serve straightaway or cover and chill briefly.

Some more ideas

● Instead of passion fruit, add 3 tbsp crème de cassis. Chill until ready to serve.

● Omit the passion fruit and instead serve the berry salad with a peach and apricot sauce: peel and purée 2 ripe peaches and flavour with 2–3 tbsp caster sugar, the juice of ¼ lemon and a dash of pure almond extract. Finely dice 8 ready-to-eat dried apricots and add to the peach purée. Serve the berries on plates in a pool of the sauce.

● Serve the berry salad spooned over vanilla frozen yogurt.

Plus points

● Comparing the same weight of each fruit, blackcurrants come out top of the table for vitamin C, with 200 mg in each 100 g (3½ oz), as compared to strawberries with 77 mg, raspberries 32 mg and blackberries 15 mg. These days vitamin C is not only recognised as essential to prevent scurvy (a condition where gums bleed, skin becomes fragile and blood vessels leak into the surrounding tissue, causing bruising), but also for maintaining the immune system and as an antioxidant, preventing the damaging processes that can lead to heart disease and cancer.

● To this feast of summer fruit, rich in dietary fibre and vitamin C, passion fruit also adds vitamin A, which is essential for healthy skin and good vision, and blackberries add vitamin E, an important antioxidant. The effects of vitamin E are enhanced by other antioxidants like vitamin C, so this combination of fruits is particularly healthy.

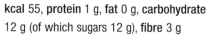

Each serving provides

kcal 55, **protein** 1 g, **fat** 0 g, **carbohydrate** 12 g (of which sugars 12 g), **fibre** 3 g

✓✓✓ C

✓ E, folate

Far Eastern fruit salad

A can of fruit can be transformed into a special-tasting fruit salad with the minimum of effort. Here, lychees are enhanced with stem ginger and the zest and juice of fresh lime for an Oriental flavour, then tossed with crisp apple, oranges and black grapes from the fruit bowl.

Serves 4

1 can lychees in syrup, about 425 g
3 pieces stem ginger, cut into fine strips, plus
    2 tbsp syrup from the jar
grated zest and juice of 1 lime
2 oranges
200 g (7 oz) black grapes, halved and seeded
1 red-skinned dessert apple, cored and
    chopped
fine shreds of lime zest to decorate

Preparation time: 15–20 minutes

1 Drain the lychees in a sieve set over a bowl. Discard half of the syrup that has drained into the bowl, then add the lychees. Stir in the stem ginger and syrup, and the lime zest and juice.

2 Cut the peel and pith away from the oranges with a sharp knife. Holding the oranges over the bowl so that all the juice will drip into the salad, carefully cut between the membrane to release the segments. Add the segments to the bowl. Squeeze the membrane and add the juice to the bowl.

3 Stir in the grapes and apple and toss to mix. Pile the salad into small bowls to serve, decorated with shreds of lime zest.

Plus points

• Black grapes provide useful amounts of bioflavonoids and antioxidants, which help to protect the body against the damaging effect of free radicals.

• Oranges are an excellent source of vitamin C – 1 large orange provides double the recommended daily amount of this vitamin. Oranges also provide useful amounts of the B vitamin folate, as well as pectin which is a type of soluble fibre.

Some more ideas

• Instead of lychees use 1 can of green figs in syrup, about 410 g, draining off half of the syrup from the can as above. Add 120 ml (4 fl oz) strained jasmine tea sweetened with 1 tbsp sugar, the lime zest and juice, and the orange segments and juice. Add the seeds and juice from 2 large passion fruit, 1 sliced banana and 4 chopped dessert plums.

• If you usually serve cream or ice-cream with a fruit salad as a dessert, you might instead try topping with a scoop of sorbet, which is deliciously fruity and fat-free. A sorbet such as lemon or mango would be particularly good with this fruit salad.

Each serving provides

kcal 150, protein 2 g, fat 0 g, carbohydrate 37 g (of which sugars 37 g), fibre 3 g

✓✓✓ C
✓ folate

Pimm's melon cup

This salad is inspired by the classic summer drink, which is often garnished with so much fruit that it is almost a fruit salad in itself. A mixture of sweet melon, berries, pear and cucumber is marinated in Pimm's and then served in melon shells. A decoration of pretty borage flowers is a traditional finish.

Serves 4

1 small Ogen melon

1 small cantaloupe or Charentais melon

200 g (7 oz) strawberries, sliced

1 pear, cut into 2.5 cm (1 in) chunks

¼ cucumber, cut into 1 cm (½ in) dice

1 carambola, cut into 5 mm (¼ in) slices

6 tbsp Pimm's

2 tbsp shredded fresh mint or lemon balm leaves

borage flowers to decorate (optional)

Preparation time: 20–25 minutes, plus 20 minutes' marinating

1 Cut the melons in half horizontally and scoop out the seeds from the centre. Using a melon baller or a small spoon, scoop out the flesh into a large bowl. Reserve the melon shells.

2 Add the sliced strawberries, pear chunks and cucumber dice to the melon in the bowl. Reserve some slices of carambola for decoration and chop the rest. Add to the bowl.

3 Sprinkle the Pimm's over the fruit. Add the shredded mint or lemon balm and stir gently to mix together. Cover with cling film and set aside in a cool place or the fridge to marinate for 20 minutes.

4 With a tablespoon scoop any odd pieces of melon flesh from the shells to make them smooth. Pile the fruit mixture into the shells and decorate with the reserved slices of carambola and borage flowers, if using.

Some more ideas

• For a non-alcoholic version, omit the Pimm's and flavour with 1–2 tsp Angostura bitters or with a cordial such as elderflower.

• Turn this into a luncheon fruit and vegetable salad, using just 1 melon (either Ogen or cantaloupe), the strawberries and cucumber plus an apple instead of the pear and 100 g (3½ oz) seedless green grapes. Omit the Pimm's. Make a bed of salad leaves, including some watercress and chopped spring onion, on each plate and pile the fruit on top. Add a scoop of plain cottage cheese and sprinkle with chopped fresh mint and toasted pine nuts.

Plus points

• This delicious combination of fresh fruit provides plenty of fibre and vitamins, especially vitamin C and beta-carotene (which is found in orange-fleshed melon varieties), both important antioxidants.

• While the latest research shows that women should avoid alcohol altogether during pregnancy, in the population as a whole moderate alcohol consumption is now associated with a lower risk of death from coronary heart disease. Moderate means avoiding binges and taking no more than 3–4 units a day for men and 2–3 units a day for women.

Each serving provides

kcal 101, **protein** 1.5 g, **fat** 0 g, **carbohydrate** 12 g (of which sugars 12 g), **fibre** 2 g

✓✓✓	C
✓✓	A
✓	folate

Apple and date salad

A crunchy salad of fruit, vegetables and nuts in a creamy yogurt-based dressing, this is attractively presented on chicory leaves, the bitterness of the chicory providing a good contrast to the sweet fruit. Enjoy it for lunch with crusty bread, or serve it as a side dish to a main meal for 6–8, to accompany smoked chicken or other poultry.

Serves 4

55 g (2 oz) hazelnuts, chopped

2 green-skinned dessert apples, cored and
  roughly chopped

170 g (6 oz) fresh dates, stoned and roughly
  chopped

1 small red pepper, seeded and chopped

2 celery sticks, sliced

115 g (4 oz) seedless green grapes, halved if
  large

2 heads red or white chicory

2 tbsp chopped parsley (optional)

Yogurt dressing

150 g (5½ oz) plain low-fat yogurt

4 tbsp mayonnaise

1 tbsp lemon juice

1 tsp caster sugar

salt and pepper

Preparation time: 15 minutes

1 Put the hazelnuts into a small dry frying pan and toast over a moderate heat, stirring, until you can smell the nutty fragrance. Tip the nuts into a bowl and set aside.

2 To make the dressing, put the yogurt, mayonnaise, lemon juice and sugar into a large bowl with salt and pepper to taste and mix well.

3 Add the apples to the bowl and stir until the pieces are well coated with the dressing. Add the dates, red pepper, celery and grapes and stir to mix.

4 Separate the heads of chicory into leaves, trimming off the hard bases. Slice the bottom half of the leaves and add to the salad. Pile the salad on a large plate or in a shallow serving dish and arrange the tops of the chicory leaves round the edge. Sprinkle over the toasted nuts and parsley, if using.

Some more ideas

• If you cannot find fresh dates use 85 g (3 oz) sultanas instead.

• With reduced-fat mayonnaise, each serving will provide 260 kcal and 13 g fat (of which 1 g is saturated fat).

• You could dress the salad with a vinaigrette instead of the mayonnaise and yogurt mixture. Mix together 3 tbsp olive oil, 1 tbsp red wine vinegar or lemon juice, ¼ tsp Dijon mustard, ¼ tsp caster sugar, and salt and pepper to taste.

Plus points

• This recipe provides plenty of dietary fibre from apples with their skins, celery, chicory and, of course, dates. Fibre is essential to keep the digestive tract healthy.

• Many foods contain natural sugars, dates being one of the major sources – 95% of their energy content comes from natural sugars. When this comes wrapped in fibre, as it is in dates, the body can control a steady release of glucose into the bloodstream. Fresh dates are also a good source of vitamin C.

• The bacteria (*Streptococcus thermophilus* and *Lactobacillus bulgaricus*) traditionally used to make yogurt are known to be helpful in maintaining the balance between the 'friendly' and 'unfriendly' bacteria that live in the digestive tract. They do so by producing lactic acid which inhibits the growth of the unfriendly bacteria that can cause ill health.

Each serving provides Ⓥ

kcal 320, **protein** 5 g, **fat** 21 g (of which saturated fat 2 g), **carbohydrate** 30 g (of which sugars 30 g), **fibre** 3 g

✓✓✓	C, E
✓✓	A
✓	B$_1$, B$_2$, B$_6$, B$_{12}$, folate, niacin, calcium, potassium

raw vitality

Cauliflower and banana salad

This unusual salad uses both sweet and tart fruit with cashew nuts to add colour and interest to pretty cauliflower florets, blanched just for a moment to retain their crispness. Roasted cumin seeds and fresh thyme marry the ensemble with their full, delightfully savoury flavours. Serve with a green vegetable or salad and bread.

Serves 4

300 g (10½ oz) tiny cauliflower florets

55 g (2 oz) cashew nuts, roughly chopped

1 tsp cumin seeds

2 tbsp fresh thyme leaves

2 bananas

juice of ½ lemon

1 tbsp olive oil

3 sharon fruit (persimmon), peeled and cut into small chunks

4 tbsp snipped fresh chives

sprigs of fresh thyme to garnish

Preparation time: 15 minutes, plus 15–30 minutes' marinating

1 Bring a saucepan of water to the boil, add the cauliflower florets and bring back to a full rolling boil. Drain immediately in a colander and refresh under cold running water. Leave to drain thoroughly.

2 Roast the cashews with the cumin seeds and thyme in a heavy-based frying pan for 30–60 seconds or until the nuts are lightly browned. Tip into a bowl and set aside to cool.

3 Slice the bananas. Put into a mixing bowl, add the lemon juice and toss to coat. Add the cauliflower florets and the nut mixture, together with the olive oil. Toss gently to mix.

4 Add the sharon fruit and chives to the salad and fold in. Cover the bowl with cling film and leave to marinate for 15–30 minutes.

5 Spoon the salad into a shallow serving dish and garnish with fresh thyme sprigs.

Another idea

● For a cauliflower, banana and walnut salad, use walnuts instead of cashews and omit the cumin seeds and sharon fruit. Add ¼ tsp ground mace, 1 spring onion, finely chopped, 100 g (3½ oz) seedless green grapes, halved, and 100 g (3½ oz) ready-to-eat dried mango, diced, with the chives in step 4.

Plus points

● In addition to the vitamins and minerals provided by this delicious combination of fruit and vegetables, the nuts provide some protein and essential fatty acids.

● Although cashews and other nuts contain a lot of fat, most of this is of the unsaturated 'healthy' kind.

● Bananas are a carbohydrate-rich fruit, popular with athletes who need to maintain muscle stores of glycogen.

● The potassium bananas provide is important for the regulation of fluid balance in the body. Getting the balance right between sodium and potassium in the diet is important in preventing high blood pressure, stroke and coronary heart disease.

Each serving provides

kcal 235, **protein** 6 g, **fat** 10 g (of which saturated fat 2 g), **carbohydrate** 32 g (of which sugars 28 g), **fibre** 4 g

✓✓ B₁, B₆, copper

✓ B₂, E, niacin, potassium, zinc

raw vitality

Watermelon and feta salad

A summery cheese salad, this has been devised with a nod towards the Mediterranean. The salty tang of creamy feta cheese is contrasted with bright pink and orange fruit, luscious and full of sweet flavour. A mix of salad leaves adds a slightly peppery taste, and toasted seeds give crunch. With bread, this is good for lunch.

Serves 6

400 g (14 oz) watermelon flesh

2 nectarines or peaches

170 g (6 oz) mixed salad leaves, including
   rocket and frisée

200 g (7 oz) feta cheese

2 tbsp extra virgin olive oil

juice of ½ lemon

salt and pepper

2 tbsp toasted pumpkin or sunflower seeds

Preparation time: 15 minutes

1 Cut the watermelon into bite-sized chunks, removing all the seeds as you come across them. Halve the nectarines or peaches and remove the stone, then slice the flesh. Tear the salad leaves into bite-sized pieces, if necessary. Combine the fruit and leaves in a large salad bowl.

2 Crumble the feta cheese over the salad. Add the oil and lemon juice and toss gently until well mixed. Season with plenty of black pepper, but add salt cautiously as the cheese can be very salty. Sprinkle over the seeds and serve.

Some more ideas

• Replace the watermelon and peaches or nectarines with 600 g (1 lb 5 oz) of pears, cored and cut into chunks, and use creamy Stilton instead of the feta cheese. Include radicchio and chicory in the mix of salad leaves.

• Wensleydale or white Cheshire cheese can be used in the watermelon version instead of feta.

• Toasted walnuts can be added to either version in place of the toasted seeds.

Plus points

• Colourful fruit provide a number of vitamins, including vitamin A from beta-carotene, which gives the yellow colour to peaches and nectarines.

• As well as protein, the cheese provides calcium. Note, though, that feta is high in sodium (salt), with more than twice as much as is found in the same quantity of Cheddar. To reduce the salt content, you can soak the feta in milk for 30 minutes beforehand.

• Toasted pumpkin and sunflower seeds contain a variety of useful minerals, including phosphorus, magnesium and copper, as well as fibre and protein. Both types of seeds are rich sources of fat, but this is mostly the healthy, unsaturated type.

• Sunflower seeds are a particularly good source of vitamin E.

Each serving provides

kcal 185, **protein** 7 g, **fat** 13 g (of which saturated fat 6 g), **carbohydrate** 9 g (of which sugars 8 g), **fibre** 1 g

✓✓	C
✓	A, B₁₂, E, folate, niacin, calcium, copper

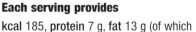

raw vitality

Tropical fruit with coriander

With its unusual combination of sweet tropical fruit and crunchy vegetables in a chilli-spiced dressing, this is a most attractive and appetising salad. Serve it as part of an al fresco meal in the summer, with grilled chicken.

Serves 4

1 red onion, halved, thinly sliced and separated into half-rings

1 ripe but firm mango

2 kiwi fruit, peeled and thinly sliced crossways

¼ cucumber, thinly sliced

Chilli and coriander dressing

1 fresh red chilli, seeded and finely chopped

2 tbsp sunflower oil

2 tbsp lime juice

1 tsp clear honey

2 tbsp chopped fresh coriander

salt and pepper

Preparation time: 15 minutes, plus 30 minutes marinating

1 Combine all the dressing ingredients in a screw-top jar, adding salt and pepper to taste. Shake well to blend.

2 Put the onion in a shallow dish, pour over the dressing and leave to marinate for 30 minutes.

3 Halve the mango lengthways, cutting down round each side of the stone. Peel off the skin, then cut the flesh into small slices and place in a bowl. Add the kiwi and cucumber.

4 Tip the marinated onion into the bowl together with all the dressing and fold together gently.

Some more ideas

• If you are not fond of the taste of coriander, try using fresh mint instead.

• Add 2 large ripe plums, cut into thin slices, and use 2 oranges instead of the mango. Peel the oranges, removing all the white pith, then cut into segments between the membranes. Squeeze all the juice from the membranes and add to the salad.

Plus points

• Kiwi fruit are an excellent source of vitamin C – weight for weight they contain more vitamin C than oranges, and one single kiwi fruit will provide almost 100% of the recommended daily amount of this vitamin. Kiwi also provide some potassium (a good intake of which may help to prevent high blood pressure) and soluble fibre (which can help to reduce high blood cholesterol levels).

• Weight for weight, chillies are also richer in vitamin C than citrus fruit, although to benefit from this you would have to eat more of them than you would probably want.

Each serving provides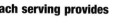

kcal 100, **protein** 1 g, **fat** 6 g (of which saturated fat 1 g), **carbohydrate** 12 g (of which sugars 11 g), **fibre** 2 g

✓✓✓ C

✓   A, E

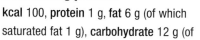

Citrus and spinach salad

In this colourful salad, the subtle flavour of spinach is enhanced by sweet melon and citrus, and Parma ham adds a savoury touch. You can prepare the dressing in advance, but only assemble the salad at the last moment to preserve as much vitamin C as possible. Serve with French or Italian bread as a light main dish.

Serves 4

1 ruby grapefruit

1 large orange

225 g (8 oz) young spinach leaves

250 g (9 oz) cantaloupe melon flesh, cut into bite-sized chunks

2 spring onions, white parts only, very thinly sliced

55 g (2 oz) thinly sliced Parma ham, excess fat removed, cut into shreds

Creamy dressing

1 tbsp best-quality balsamic vinegar

1 tbsp extra virgin olive oil

1 tbsp single cream

½ tsp honey

salt and pepper

Preparation time: 15 minutes

Each serving provides

kcal 115, **protein** 5 g, **fat** 5 g (of which saturated fat 1 g), **carbohydrate** 13 g (of which sugars 12 g), **fibre** 3 g

✓✓✓ A, C, folate

✓ B₁, B₆, niacin, calcium, iron

1 To make the dressing, put the vinegar, oil, cream and honey in a small screw-top jar. Cover and shake until well blended. Set aside.

2 Working over a bowl to catch the juice, peel the grapefruit, removing all the bitter white pith, then cut it into segments between the membranes. If large, cut the segments into bite-sized pieces. Set the grapefruit segments aside on a plate.

3 Using a citrus zester, take fine shreds of zest from the orange and set aside. Working over the bowl containing the grapefruit juice, peel the orange, removing all the pith, then cut it into segments between the membranes and cut the segments into bite-sized pieces, if liked. Add to the grapefruit segments and set aside.

4 Add 1 tbsp of the combined grapefruit and orange juices to the dressing and shake again to blend. Taste and add more citrus juice, if liked. Add salt and pepper to taste.

5 Place the spinach in a large serving bowl. Add the orange and grapefruit segments, the melon and spring onions and toss together. Shake the dressing once more, then pour it over the salad and toss. Scatter the Parma ham and orange zest over the top and serve at once.

Plus points

- This salad is a first-class source of vitamin C. The fruit are loaded with this essential vitamin, as is the spinach. Vitamin C is destroyed when food is cooked or cut, which is why it is better to leave the spinach leaves whole.
- Ruby and pink grapefruit contain the antioxidant beta-carotene, which is converted into vitamin A by the body.

Some more ideas

- To add a peppery flavour, replace 55 g (2 oz) of the spinach with watercress leaves removed from their stalks. Watercress is an excellent source of vitamin C, as well as beta-carotene.
- Replace the balsamic vinegar with a fruit-flavoured vinegar, such as raspberry or lemon.
- Make this into a vegetarian salad by omitting the Parma ham. If you want to retain the flavour contrast of the fruit with a savoury, salty ingredient, sprinkle the salad with 55 g (2 oz) of drained and crumbled feta cheese.

raw vitality

Savoury Ways with Fruit

Main dishes with an unexpected zing

USING FRUIT IN SAVOURY MAIN DISHES is a clever and easy way to increase your daily fruit intake. All kinds of fruit – fresh or dried – can be used, each adding its own flavour, texture and colour to a dish, as well as essential vitamins, minerals and fibre. Put pineapple into a creamy curry with juicy tiger prawns, figs into a succulent lamb stew spiced with star anise, or apricots into a family-style chicken casserole. Grill Asian pears with marinated pork chops. Or why not toss mango into a Thai-style stir-fry of steak, or mix apple into lamb burgers?

Malaysian prawns and pineapple

This is really quick to make, yet very authentic-tasting. Although creamed coconut is a rich source of fat, this recipe uses much less than is usually found in Malaysian and Thai recipes. Serve with rice noodles or rice.

Serves 4

2 onions, roughly chopped

2 garlic cloves

2 tbsp sunflower oil

1 large fresh red chilli, halved, seeded and thinly sliced

1 tsp ground cumin

1 tsp white pepper

1 tsp turmeric

2 tsp ground coriander

450 ml (15 fl oz) fish stock

2 tbsp fish sauce

1 tbsp soft brown sugar

55 g (2 oz) creamed coconut

500 g (1 lb 2 oz) raw tiger prawns

250 g (9 oz) fresh pineapple flesh, cored and chopped

2–3 spring onions, cut into short lengths, then shredded

seeds of 1 pomegranate to garnish

Preparation time: 15 minutes

Cooking time: 25 minutes

Each serving provides

kcal 275, **protein** 18 g, **fat** 16 g (of which saturated fat 9 g), **carbohydrate** 15 g (of which sugars 14 g), **fibre** 1 g

✓✓✓	B_{12}, E
✓✓	C, niacin, copper, iron
✓	B_1, B_2, B_6, calcium, potassium, selenium, zinc

1 Tip the onions and peeled garlic into a food processor and process to a smooth purée. Alternatively, very finely chop the onions and garlic with a sharp knife.

2 Heat the oil in a large non-stick pan and fry the onion mixture for about 10 minutes or until softened and beginning to colour. Stir occasionally towards the end of the cooking time to prevent the mixture from sticking.

3 Add the chilli and all of the spices to the pan and stir to mix with the onions. Pour in the fish stock and add the fish sauce, sugar and creamed coconut. Mix well. Cover and leave to simmer gently for 10 minutes.

4 Meanwhile, peel the tiger prawns, leaving the last tail section on each one, if you like.

5 Stir the prawns into the sauce and cook very gently, uncovered, for 3–4 minutes or until they turn from bluey-grey to pink. Take care not to overcook or they will toughen.

6 Stir in the pineapple and spring onions. Cook for just 1 minute to warm the pineapple through. Sprinkle with the pomegranate seeds, and serve.

Plus points

• Prawns are an excellent source of vitamin B_{12} and a good source of selenium which works with vitamin E to promote normal body growth and fertility. As an antioxidant selenium is also believed to help in the fight against cancer.

• Onions and garlic are not just a valuable asset in the kitchen, they have been used throughout history as a cure-all. Recent research suggests that they lower blood cholesterol and so reduce the risk of coronary heart disease. They also prevent blood clotting and are a natural decongestant. So include onions and garlic in your cooking as much as possible.

Some more ideas

• For a spicy fish satay, replace the prawns with 450 g (1 lb) skinless cod fillet, cut into cubes, and substitute crunchy peanut butter for the creamed coconut.

• Many supermarkets stock Thai fish sauce in their ethnic range, but if you can't track it down you can use a light soy sauce instead.

savoury ways with fruit

68

Chicken with apricots and cumin

Chicken thighs are excellent in a casserole, being very tender and full of flavour. Fresh apricots and a bulb of fennel make good partners, especially when spiced up with cumin. Plain boiled rice, or saffron rice (see the recipe on page 74), would be a good accompaniment, as would boiled new potatoes or baked potatoes.

Serves 4

2 tbsp sunflower oil

8 chicken thighs, about 450 g (1 lb) in total

1 onion, sliced

2 garlic cloves, chopped

2 tsp ground cumin

2 tsp ground coriander

300 ml (10 fl oz) chicken stock

3 carrots, halved crossways, then each half cut into 6–8 thick fingers

1 bulb of fennel, halved lengthways, then cut crossways into slices

300 g (10½ oz) ripe but firm apricots, stoned and quartered

salt and pepper

chopped fennel leaves from the bulb, or herb fennel, to garnish

Preparation time: 15 minutes

Cooking time: 50 minutes

1 Heat the oil in a large flameproof casserole and fry the chicken thighs for 5–10 minutes, turning occasionally, until golden brown all over. Remove from the pan. Add the onion and garlic to the casserole and fry for 5 minutes or until soft and golden.

2 Stir in all the spices and fry for 1 minute, then add the stock. Return the chicken to the casserole together with the carrots and fennel. Bring to the boil. Stir well, then cover and simmer gently for 30 minutes or until the chicken is tender. Remove the lid. If there is too much liquid, boil to reduce it slightly.

3 Add the apricots to the casserole and stir gently to mix. Simmer over a low heat for a further 5 minutes.

4 Season to taste with salt and pepper. Sprinkle with the fennel leaves and serve with rice or potatoes.

Plus points

- Chicken is a good source of protein.
- Both apricots and carrots provide some vitamin A in the form of beta-carotene, which gives them their distinctive colour, but carrots are by far the better source, providing about 20 times more of this nutrient per 100 g (3½ oz) than apricots. Vitamin A is essential for proper vision and increasingly valued for its role as an antioxidant, helping to prevent cancer and coronary heart disease.

Some more ideas

- Most of the fat in chicken is contained in the skin, so removing the skin before cooking will reduce the calories per serving to 310 kcal and the fat content per serving to 16 g, of which 3 g is saturated fat.
- For a different flavour, omit the ground cumin and coriander and add 8 tbsp black bean sauce at the end of step 3 and heat through.
- Replace the apricots with 1 fresh mango, cut into slices or chunks. Sprinkle with fresh coriander instead of fennel leaves.
- Use 1 can of apricot halves in natural juice, about 400 g, drained and cut in half, instead of fresh apricots.

Each serving provides

kcal 370, **protein** 26 g, **fat** 24 g (of which saturated fat 6 g), **carbohydrate** 12 g (of which sugars 11 g), **fibre** 4 g

✓✓✓	A
✓✓	B₆, C
✓	B₁, B₂, folate, copper, iron, potassium, selenium, zinc

Chicken and banana korma

This mild chicken and banana curry, enriched with almonds and yogurt, has a wonderfully smooth, creamy texture. Boneless, skinless chicken thighs add plenty of flavour, while being convenient to eat, quick to cook and quite low in fat. Serve with basmati rice and crispy grilled poppadoms or naan bread.

Serves 4

1 large mild onion, roughly chopped

1 large fresh red chilli, seeded

5 cm (2 in) piece fresh root ginger, chopped

3 garlic cloves

2 tbsp sunflower oil

1 tbsp garam masala

450 ml (15 fl oz) chicken stock

55 g (2 oz) ground almonds

8 skinless boneless chicken thighs, about
    450 g (1 lb) in total

150 g (5½ oz) plain low-fat yogurt

2 tsp cornflour

2 large bananas

2 tbsp chopped fresh coriander, plus extra to
    garnish

2 tbsp toasted flaked almonds (optional)

Lime and apple raita

grated zest and juice of ½ lime

2 red-skinned apples, cored and roughly
    chopped

1 small red onion or 2 shallots, finely chopped

2 tbsp finely chopped fresh coriander

Preparation time: 15–20 minutes

Cooking time: 40 minutes

1 Put the onion, chilli, ginger and peeled garlic in a food processor and process to a smooth purée. Alternatively, very finely chop the onion, chilli, ginger and garlic with a sharp knife.

2 Heat the oil in a large non-stick pan and fry the onion mixture for about 10 minutes or until softened, stirring more frequently towards the end of the cooking time to prevent the mixture from sticking.

3 Add the garam masala and stir to mix. Pour in the stock and stir in the ground almonds. Add the chicken thighs. Cover the pan and leave to simmer gently for 25 minutes.

4 Meanwhile, take 1 tbsp of the yogurt and place in a bowl with all the ingredients for the lime and apple raita. Stir to mix. Set aside.

5 Mix the cornflour into the remaining yogurt. Add this mixture to the curry and simmer, stirring constantly, until thickened.

6 Peel and slice the bananas, then add to the curry with the chopped coriander. Cook for just a few more minutes to warm the bananas. Serve the curry hot, sprinkled with chopped coriander and the toasted almonds, if using, with the raita alongside.

Plus points

• Almonds are a source of fibre, vitamin E and several minerals. They are also high in fat, although 87% of it is unsaturated.

• Both bananas and apples provide fibre, and bananas are also a useful source of potassium, with 10% RNI in one fruit.

Some more ideas

• For a turkey and mango korma, replace the chicken with 450 g (1 lb) skinless turkey breast steaks, cut into cubes. At the end of the cooking time add 1 fresh mango, peeled and cut into cubes, and 1–2 tbsp mango chutney in place of the bananas.

• For a banana raita, replace the apples with 2 chopped bananas. For extra heat, add ½ small fresh red chilli, finely chopped.

Each serving provides

kcal 500, **protein** 37 g, **fat** 24 g (of which saturated fat 4 g), **carbohydrate** 35 g (of which sugars 27 g), **fibre** 4 g

✓✓✓	B$_{12}$, zinc
✓✓	C, B$_2$, B$_6$, E, copper, potassium, selenium
✓	B$_1$, folate, niacin, calcium, iron

savoury ways with fruit

72

Lamb and fig stew with star anise

Meat and fruit is a classic combination in many cuisines, all over the world. This slowly cooked stew of tender lamb and sweet dried figs, flavoured with warm spices, is a superb partnership of meat and fruit, ideal for a special occasion. The stew is served with golden-yellow saffron rice for a delightful colour contrast.

Serves 4

2 tbsp olive oil

2 large garlic cloves, crushed

340 g (12 oz) onions, sliced

550 g (1¼ lb) boneless leg of lamb, well trimmed and cut into 5 cm (2 in) cubes

150 g (5½ oz) ready-to-eat dried figs

1½ tbsp grated fresh root ginger

1 cinnamon stick, broken in half

2 star anise

340 g (12 oz) carrots, chopped

340 g (12 oz) courgettes, chopped

chilli sauce to taste

salt and pepper

large handful of mixed fresh parsley and coriander, finely chopped

Saffron rice

340 g (12 oz) basmati rice, well rinsed

good pinch of saffron threads

1¼ tsp salt

Preparation time: about 20 minutes
Cooking time: about 2 hours

Each serving provides

kcal 715, **protein** 38 g, **fat** 18 g (of which saturated fat 1 g), **carbohydrate** 102 g (of which sugars 31 g), **fibre** 6 g

✓✓✓	A, B₆, B₁₂, niacin, iron, zinc
✓✓	B₁, C, folate, potassium
✓	B₂, calcium, copper

1 Heat the olive oil in a flameproof casserole or large heavy-based saucepan over a moderate heat. Add the garlic and fry for 1 minute, stirring frequently, then add the onions and stir to coat with the oil. Turn the heat to low, put a piece of dampened greaseproof paper on top of the onions and cover with a tight-fitting lid. Cook for 20 minutes or until the onions are very tender and sweet.

2 Add the lamb to the casserole. Pour in 1.2 litres (2 pints) of water or enough to cover the lamb and onions. Increase the heat and bring to the boil, skimming to remove any foam. Reduce the heat to low. Add the figs, ginger, cinnamon and star anise. Cover and simmer for 1 hour or until the meat is very tender.

3 Meanwhile, for the saffron rice, put the rice in a bowl, add water to cover by 2.5 cm (1 in) and leave to soak for 30 minutes. Drain the rice well and set aside.

4 Heat a dry frying pan over a high heat, add the saffron threads and toast for 30 seconds or until they give off their aroma. Immediately tip them out of the pan into a measuring jug and pour in 450 ml (15 fl oz) of boiling water. Stir to mix, then set aside to infuse for at least 30 minutes.

5 When the lamb is tender, use a draining spoon to remove it from the casserole and set aside. Remove the star anise and cinnamon stick and discard. Transfer half the liquid, onions and figs from the casserole to a food processor or blender and process until smooth. Stir this mixture back into the casserole to thicken the sauce. Alternatively, remove the lamb and discard the spices, then use a hand-held blender to purée some of the onions and figs in the casserole. Stir well.

6 Return the lamb to the casserole and add the carrots. Bring to the boil, then reduce the heat and simmer for 10 minutes.

7 Add the courgettes and continue simmering for 5 minutes or until both vegetables are tender but still crisp. Then leave to cook over a low heat while you finish the rice (cover the pan if you do not want the sauce to become any thicker, or leave uncovered if you want to reduce it a bit more).

8 To cook the rice, bring the saffron-infused water to the boil in a heavy-based saucepan and add the salt. Tip in the rice and bring back to the boil, then reduce the heat to low, cover the pan and simmer for 10 minutes. Remove from the heat and leave, still covered, for 5 minutes.

savoury ways with fruit

9 Taste the lamb stew and stir in chilli sauce, salt and pepper to taste. Sprinkle with the chopped parsley and coriander, and serve immediately, with the saffron rice on the side.

Some more ideas

• Replace the dried figs with dried apricots or dried dates.

• To make a vegetarian version of this dish, replace the lamb with drained and rinsed canned beans, such as chickpeas or butter beans. Use 2 cans, about 400 g each. After the onions have cooked for 20 minutes, add the figs, spices and water, and simmer for about 30 minutes to blend the flavours. Add the beans with the courgettes.

Plus points

• Although lamb still tends to contain more fat than other meats, changes in breeding, feeding and butchery techniques mean that lean cuts only contain about one-third of the fat they would have 20 years ago. More of the fat is monounsaturated, which is good news for healthy hearts.

Pork chops with Asian pears

Try this easy dish with Oriental flavourings as an alternative to traditional roast pork with sweetened apple sauce. The carbohydrate-rich rice includes mildly sweet Asian pears. You will find Asian pears in many supermarkets as well as in Chinese food shops. They look like large apples and have a crisp texture.

Serves 4

4 boneless pork loin chops, about 140 g
  (5 oz) each, well trimmed of fat
1 Asian pear, peeled, cored and cut into rings
sprigs of fresh coriander to garnish

Marinade

4 tbsp orange juice
2 tbsp soy sauce
1 tbsp bottled hoisin sauce
1 tbsp ginger wine

Spiced rice

340 g (12 oz) basmati rice
2 star anise
2 cloves
2 thin slices fresh root ginger, peeled
20 g (¾ oz) butter
1 tbsp sunflower oil
1¼ tsp salt
pepper
2 Asian pears, about 170 g (6 oz) each,
  peeled, cored and chopped
2–3 tbsp finely chopped fresh coriander

Preparation time: 20 minutes, plus at least
  1 hour for marinating, soaking and infusing
Cooking time: 15–20 minutes

1 To make the marinade, mix the orange juice, soy sauce, hoisin sauce and ginger wine together in a dish large enough to hold the pork chops in a single layer. Add the chops and turn to coat on both sides. Cover with cling film. Marinate in the fridge for at least 1 hour or, preferably, up to 12 hours.

2 To prepare the rice, rinse it in a sieve under cold running water until the water runs clear. Place in a bowl, add water to cover by 2.5 cm (1 in) and leave to soak for 30 minutes.

3 Put the star anise, cloves and ginger in a small saucepan with 450 ml (15 fl oz) of water and bring to the boil. Remove from the heat, cover and set aside to infuse for 30 minutes.

4 Preheat the grill to high. Lightly oil the grill rack.

5 Using a spoon, remove the spices from the water and bring the water back to the boil. Drain the rice well. Melt the butter with the oil in a heavy-based saucepan. Add the rice and stir until it is well coated. Pour in the spice-infused water and add the salt and pepper to taste. When the water returns to the boil, reduce the heat to low. Stir in the chopped Asian pears. Cover the pan and leave to simmer for 10 minutes. Remove from the heat and leave undisturbed for about 5 minutes.

6 While the rice is cooking, remove the pork chops from the marinade, letting the excess marinade drip back into the dish. Place the chops on the grill rack and grill for 10 minutes, basting with the reserved marinade.

7 Turn the chops over and add the Asian pear rings to the grill rack. Brush the chops and pear rings with the reserved marinade. Continue grilling and basting for a further 5–7 minutes or until the chops are cooked (the juices should run clear when a chop is pierced with the tip of a sharp knife). Turn the pear rings over half way through the cooking time.

8 Uncover the rice and stir in the chopped coriander. Taste and adjust the seasoning, if necessary. Serve each chop with a large portion of the spiced rice, garnished with the grilled pear rings and sprigs of coriander.

Each serving provides

kcal 670, **protein** 54 g, **fat** 16 g (of which saturated fat 6 g), **carbohydrate** 77 g (of which sugars 9 g), **fibre** 2 g

---

✓✓✓ B$_1$, B$_6$, B$_{12}$, niacin

✓ B$_2$, E, copper, iron, potassium, selenium, zinc

Some more ideas

• Replace the pork chops with 4 skinless boneless chicken breasts, weighing about 140 g (5 oz) each. Marinate the chicken breasts as in the recipe, then grill for 6 minutes on each side or until the juices run clear when the chicken is pierced with the tip of a knife. Replace the spiced water for the rice with chicken stock.

• For a Mediterranean flavour, make the marinade with 120 ml (4 fl oz) dry red wine, 1 large garlic clove, crushed, 4 fresh sage leaves, torn into pieces, and 2 finely pared strips of lemon zest. For the rice, omit the spices and replace the Asian pears with 2 peeled and finely chopped peaches. Stir in chopped fresh parsley rather than coriander just before serving.

Plus points

• Pork is a good source of protein, as well as iron and B vitamins.

• Despite its rather 'fatty' image, these days the fat content of lean pork is around 4%, which is lower than that of beef or lamb.

Prune and Parma ham kebabs with apricot sauce

Prunes wrapped in Parma ham are threaded onto skewers with onions and yellow peppers, and served with a piquant apricot sauce and a spicy bulghur wheat pilaf. All that is needed to complete the meal is a green salad.

Serves 4

8–12 slices Parma ham, about 115 g (4 oz) in total

24 large ready-to-eat prunes, stoned

4 small onions, about 340 g (12 oz) in total, each cut into 6 wedges

2 yellow peppers, seeded and cut into 24 large cubes

2 tbsp sunflower oil

shredded spring onion greens to garnish

Apricot sauce

1 can apricot halves in natural juice, about 400 g

2 spring onions, chopped

½ tsp ground cumin

1 tsp soy sauce

1 tsp balsamic vinegar

Bulghur pilaf

225 g (8 oz) bulghur wheat

2 tbsp sunflower oil

1 onion, chopped

1 garlic clove, chopped

2 celery sticks, chopped

2 tsp ground cumin

8 ready-to-eat prunes, stoned and roughly chopped

Preparation time: 30 minutes
Cooking time: 20–25 minutes

1 Cut each slice of Parma ham in half, or into thirds if large, and wrap a piece round each prune. Thread onto 8 skewers alternating with the onion wedges and pepper cubes.

2 To make the sauce, put the apricots with their juice, the spring onions and cumin in a saucepan. Bring just to the boil, then simmer for 5 minutes. Pour into a food processor or blender and blend until smooth. Stir in the soy sauce and vinegar. Set aside.

3 To make the pilaf, pour boiling water over the bulghur wheat and leave to soak for 15 minutes. Meanwhile, heat the oil in a frying pan and gently fry the onion, garlic and celery for 7–8 minutes or until softened, stirring occasionally. Add the cumin and fry for 1 minute. Drain the bulghur in a sieve, pressing out as much liquid as possible. Add to the frying pan together with the chopped prunes. Stir to mix, and heat through. Keep warm.

4 Preheat the grill to high. Brush the kebabs with the oil and cook for 3–4 minutes on each side. Meanwhile, reheat the apricot sauce. Serve 2 kebabs per person with the bulghur wheat pilaf and apricot sauce, and a garnish of shredded spring onion greens.

Plus points

- Bulghur wheat is not only a good source of fibre, but like many cereals it also provides B vitamins: 100 g (3½ oz) contains three times the RNI for vitamin B_1 and two and a half times the RNI for niacin.
- Prunes provide plenty of fibre as well as some iron. The vitamin C from the apricots in the sauce will help the body to absorb the iron.

Another idea

- Replace the prunes in the kebabs with ready-to-eat dried apricots and use red peppers instead of yellow ones. Add 170 g (6 oz) cooked peas to the pilaf with the bulghur wheat, plus ½ tsp ground cinnamon with the ground cumin. If you like, garnish with chopped fresh mint.

Each serving provides

kcal 640, **protein** 17 g, **fat** 14 g (of which saturated fat 2 g), **carbohydrate** 115 g (of which sugars 69 g), **fibre** 12 g

✓✓✓	B_1, B_6, C, copper, iron, potassium
✓✓	B_2, E, niacin
✓	folate, calcium, zinc

Thai-style stir-fried beef with mango

This colourful dish is bursting with fresh flavours and deliciously contrasting textures. The dressing is completely oil-free, so although both the beef and nuts contain fat and the beef is stir-fried in a little oil, the dish is still light on the fat front. Also, no extra salt is needed because of the spicy dressing and saltiness of soy sauce.

Serves 4

400 g (14 oz) lean steak, such as sirloin

3 garlic cloves, finely chopped

1 tsp caster sugar

2 tsp soy sauce

1½ tbsp sunflower oil

Ginger and honey dressing

2 tsp paprika

2 tsp mild Mexican-style chilli powder

1½ tbsp clear honey

2.5 cm (1 in) piece fresh root ginger, grated

4 tbsp rice vinegar or cider vinegar

juice of 1 lime or lemon

Salad

1 ripe but firm mango, peeled and cut into
   strips

2 ripe but firm plums, sliced

¼ medium-sized red cabbage, shredded

55 g (2 oz) watercress leaves

½ cucumber, cut into matchsticks

½ red pepper, cut into thin strips

3–4 spring onions, cut into diagonal pieces

45 g (1½ oz) mixed fresh mint and coriander

2 tbsp coarsely chopped roasted unsalted
   peanuts

Preparation time: 30 minutes

Cooking time: about 10 minutes

1 To make the dressing, put the paprika, chilli powder, honey, ginger and vinegar in a saucepan and slowly add 250 ml (8½ fl oz) of water, stirring. Bring to the boil, then reduce the heat and simmer for 5 minutes. Remove from the heat and stir in the lime or lemon juice. Set aside.

2 Combine all the salad ingredients, except the peanuts, in a large shallow serving dish and toss gently together until evenly mixed. Set aside.

3 Cut the steak into thin strips for stir-frying. Put the steak in a bowl with the garlic, sugar and soy sauce and mix together so the strips of steak are seasoned. Heat a wok or non-stick pan on a high heat, then add the oil. Add the beef and stir-fry until the strips are evenly browned and cooked to taste.

4 Spoon the stir-fried beef over the top of the salad. Drizzle the dressing over the top and sprinkle with the peanuts. Serve immediately.

Some more ideas

• Add cubes of fresh or canned pineapple (canned in juice rather than syrup) or kiwi fruit to the salad, to increase the fruit content.

• Spice up the salad with very thin strips of fresh red chilli – particularly if you have a cold, as scientists have suggested that eating chillies can help to alleviate nasal congestion.

• Replace the mango with 2 nectarines, unpeeled and sliced.

• For a vegetarian version, omit the stir-fried beef and increase the quantity of peanuts to 150 g (5½ oz). Peanuts are an excellent source of protein and contain much less saturated fat than meat.

Plus points

• All orange and red fruit and vegetables, such as mango, red cabbage and red peppers, are excellent sources of beta-carotene and vitamin C – both antioxidants that help to protect against heart disease and cancer. The vitamin C aids the absorption of valuable iron from the steak.

• Apart from adding its delicious spiciness to the dressing, ginger also aids digestion.

Each serving provides

kcal 265, **protein** 27 g, **fat** 8 g (of which saturated fat 3 g), **carbohydrate** 20 g (of which sugars 18 g), **fibre** 3 g

✓✓✓	B₁₂, C
✓✓	A, B₆, iron, zinc
✓	B₁, B₂, E, folate, niacin, copper

Fruited lamb kofta

The variety of spices and fresh and dried fruit bring delicious flavour to these minced lamb burgers, called kofta. A beaten egg and Granary breadcrumbs bind the mixture together – the whole grains in the bread add a nutty, earthy quality, as well as fibre and B vitamins.

Serves 4 (makes 8 patties)

1 apple
½ quince
1 small onion
280 g (10 oz) lean minced lamb
3 garlic cloves, chopped
2 tbsp plain low-fat yogurt
4 tbsp chopped fresh coriander
2 tsp ground cumin
2 tsp paprika
½ tsp curry powder (mild or hot, to taste)
½ tsp ground ginger
large pinch of dried chilli flakes
¾ tsp salt, or to taste
85 g (3 oz) sultanas or raisins
2 heaped tbsp pine nuts
2 slices Granary bread, crumbled
1 egg, beaten
1 tbsp sunflower oil

Preparation time: 20–25 minutes
Cooking time: 10–15 minutes

Each serving provides

kcal 380, **protein** 20 g, **fat** 20 g (of which saturated fat 6 g), **carbohydrate** 30 g (of which sugars 21 g), **fibre** 2 g

✓✓✓	B₁₂
✓✓	copper, iron, zinc
✓	B₁, B₂, B₆, C, E, folate, niacin, calcium, potassium

1 Finely chop the apple, quince and onion using a sharp knife or in a food processor. Turn into a large bowl and add all the remaining ingredients except the oil. Knead the mixture together thoroughly with your hands. Divide into 8 portions and shape each one into a flattish cake or burger. Cover the kofta and keep in the fridge until ready to cook.

2 Heat the oil in a non-stick frying pan and fry the kofta for 5–6 minutes on each side or until golden brown. They are quite fragile because of their high fruit and moisture content, so take care when you turn them over that they do not fall apart.

3 Serve with pitta bread and plain low-fat yogurt. A red cabbage relish also goes well with this (see Some more ideas, right).

Plus points

• There are lots of good things in these kofta, including iron and fibre in the sultanas or raisins, and fibre and vitamin C in the apple and quince.
• The red cabbage relish provides plenty of vitamin C, which helps the body to absorb the iron provided by the lamb and sultanas.

Some more ideas

• Use a fresh peach or 2 dried peach halves instead of the quince.
• To make a red cabbage relish to serve with the kofta, mix together 2 tbsp sunflower oil, 1 tbsp white wine vinegar, the juice of ½ lemon, the grated zest and juice of 1 orange, 1 tbsp caster sugar, ½ fresh red chilli, seeded and finely chopped, and 1 garlic clove, finely chopped. Add ½ medium-sized red cabbage, finely shredded, and toss in the dressing.
• For a fruited vegetarian burger, use 250 g (9 oz) cooked red split lentils (drained canned lentils are fine), 60 g (2¼ oz) chickpea flour, 100 g (3½ oz) fresh breadcrumbs, 85 g (3 oz) grated mature Cheddar cheese, 30 g (1 oz) coarsely chopped unsalted peanuts, 2 tsp curry powder, ½ tsp each ground cumin and ginger, 2 tbsp each chopped fresh coriander and fresh mint, 1 small onion, finely chopped, 1 red pepper, diced, 1 apple, cored and diced, 1 pear, cored and diced, and 2 tbsp currants. Bind the mixture with 1 beaten egg. Shape into thick, plump burgers, patting firmly. Fry in 1 tbsp sunflower oil in a non-stick pan. Once the burgers are browned, they may still be a bit moist inside, so arrange them in a baking dish and bake in a 180°C (350°F, gas mark 4) oven for 10–15 minutes or until they firm up and dry out a little. Serve with the red cabbage relish or with mango chutney.

savoury ways with fruit

Braised roots with Hunza apricots

Orange juice and caramel-tasting Hunza apricots enhance a comforting mix of traditional root vegetables. This can be served as a light main course, or a side dish for 4, providing warming nourishment on cold winter days.

Serves 2

100 g (3½ oz) dried Hunza apricots
100 g (3½ oz) shallots
100 g (3½ oz) carrots
100 g (3½ oz) swede
100 g (3½ oz) turnips
100 g (3½ oz) celeriac
100 g (3½ oz) parsnips
100 g (3½ oz) sweet potato
100 g (3½ oz) mushrooms
2 tbsp olive oil
200 ml (7 fl oz) vegetable stock
200 ml (7 fl oz) orange juice
black pepper
fresh flat-leaf parsley to garnish

Preparation time: 20 minutes, plus overnight
     soaking
Cooking time: about 1 hour

Each serving provides   Ⓥ
kcal 380, **protein** 8 g, **fat** 14 g (of which
saturated fat 2 g), **carbohydrate** 59 g (of
which sugars 47 g), **fibre** 14 g

✓✓✓	A, B$_1$, C, potassium
✓✓	B$_6$, folate, niacin, calcium, copper, iron
✓	B$_2$

1 Rinse the Hunza apricots to remove any grit, then place them in a bowl and cover generously with cold water. Leave them to soak for about 8 hours or overnight until rehydrated.

2 Preheat the oven to 180°C (350°F, gas mark 4). Pull apart the shallots, allowing them to fall into their natural segments. If the shallots are large and not segmented, halve them lengthways. Cut the carrots, swede and turnips into 5 cm (2 in) chunks. Cut the celeriac, parsnips and sweet potato into 6 cm (2½ in) chunks. Quarter or halve the mushrooms, depending on size.

3 Heat the oil in a large flameproof casserole and add all of the vegetables, stirring to coat them lightly with the oil. Cook over a high heat, stirring frequently, for 5–10 minutes or until the vegetables are browned.

4 Meanwhile, drain the apricots thoroughly. Using your fingers, tear each apricot open to remove the stone and divide the flesh into quarters.

5 Pour the vegetable stock and orange juice into the casserole and bring to the boil. Add the apricots and season with pepper. Transfer the casserole to the oven and bake for 45–60 minutes or until the vegetables are tender and the liquid has reduced to a reasonably thick sauce. Garnish with parsley and serve, with crusty bread.

Some more ideas

● To make a spicier vegetarian main course dish, add 2 tsp ground cumin and 1 tsp garam masala to the oil before adding the vegetables. Add a drained can of chickpeas, about 425 g, to the casserole before adding the stock. The chickpeas will add protein.

● Onions, cut into wedges, can be used in place of the shallots and canned chopped tomatoes can be used instead of the orange juice. If desired, beef or chicken stock can be used instead of vegetable stock.

● Dried apricots can be used instead of Hunza apricots, but will give a sweeter flavour.

Plus points

● Root vegetables are generally good sources of fibre. Carrots also provide vitamin A as beta-carotene, which is essential for night vision and an important antioxidant.

● People in Hunza, a region in northern Kashmir, are famous for their long lives – and some have put this down to eating apricots. Whether true or not, dried apricots are a good source of fibre and iron and a useful source of vitamin A.

savoury ways with fruit

Moroccan vegetable tagine

Even meat-eaters will love this flavour-packed vegetable stew. The slightly tart taste of dried cherries combines with sweet, plump raisins in a spicy mixture of chunky vegetables, chickpeas and ginger. Despite the long list of ingredients, the stew is simple to prepare for a hearty family meal.

Serves 4

2 tbsp olive oil

1 large red onion, very roughly chopped

4 garlic cloves, sliced

1 tbsp shredded fresh root ginger

550 g (1¼ lb) butternut squash, peeled, seeded and cubed

1 tsp ground cinnamon

1 tsp ground cumin

1 tsp ground coriander

6 green cardamom pods, split open and seeds lightly crushed

3 bay leaves

2 cans chopped tomatoes, about 400 g each

225 g (8 oz) large carrots, very thickly sliced

300 ml (10 fl oz) boiling vegetable stock

55 g (2 oz) raisins

30 g (1 oz) dried cherries

125 g (4½ oz) okra, sliced lengthways into 3

1 large red pepper, roughly chopped

1 can chickpeas, about 425 g, drained

30 g (1 oz) toasted flaked almonds

3 tbsp chopped fresh flat-leaf parsley

Spicy couscous

340 g (12 oz) couscous

450 ml (15 fl oz) boiling vegetable stock

1 tbsp olive oil

1 tsp chilli sauce such as harissa

½ tsp ground coriander

½ tsp ground cumin

Preparation time: 25 minutes

Cooking time: 30 minutes

1 Heat the oil in a very large pan and stir-fry the onion over a high heat for 2–3 minutes or until beginning to soften and colour. Toss in the garlic and ginger and cook for a few more seconds. Tip in the squash and stir-fry for about 1 minute.

2 Turn down the heat. Add all of the spices, the bay leaves, tomatoes and carrots. Pour in the boiling stock. Stir in the raisins and cherries, then cover and simmer for 10 minutes.

3 Meanwhile, prepare the couscous. Tip the couscous into a large bowl and pour in the boiling stock. Add the oil, chilli sauce and spices. Leave until the liquid has been completely absorbed, then fork the mixture through to separate the grains. Tip into a colander lined with greaseproof paper.

4 Stir the okra and red pepper into the stew, then cover and leave to simmer for 5 minutes. Add the chickpeas and stir. Set the colander containing the couscous over the pan and simmer for a further 5–10 minutes or until all the vegetables are tender but still retain their shape and texture and the couscous is hot.

5 Tip the couscous onto a platter. Pile the vegetable stew on top of the couscous and scatter over the toasted almonds and chopped parsley.

Plus points

• Beans and chickpeas are an excellent source of protein, even better when they are eaten with grains such as wheat (couscous) and rice. Canned versions are a convenient way of including them in the diet with the minimum of effort.

Some more ideas

• For an apricot and coriander tagine, replace the cherries and raisins with ready-to-eat dried apricots, use halved French beans instead of the okra, and substitute fresh coriander for the parsley. Add 2 tbsp chopped fresh coriander to the tagine at the end of the cooking time as well as scattering some over the finished dish.

• Whole new potatoes can replace the carrots.

• Red kidney beans can be used as an alternative to the chickpeas, or instead of adding them to the tagine toss them into the couscous for added texture.

Each serving provides

kcal 670, **protein** 24 g, **fat** 17 g (of which saturated fat 2 g), **carbohydrate** 110 g (of which sugars 35 g), **fibre** 14 g

✓✓✓	A, B$_1$, C, folate, copper
✓✓	B$_6$, niacin, calcium, iron
✓	B$_2$, E, zinc

savoury ways with fruit

Mexican beans and fruit

Earthy, rustic beans are surprisingly good paired with fruit, as in this classic from the Mexican kitchen, where it is called frijoles con frutas. *If fruit with beans sounds alarming, just remember that the tomato – an essential ingredient of our familiar baked beans – is also a fruit. This is a high-fibre dish, rich with vitamins.*

Serves 4

½ medium-sized to large pineapple
2 green-skinned apples, such as Granny
   Smith
juice of ½ lemon
2 tbsp sunflower oil
2 onions, chopped
3 garlic cloves, chopped
3 ripe tomatoes, preferably plum tomatoes,
   diced
1 tsp hot chilli powder or Tabasco sauce, or
   more to taste
2 cans borlotti beans, about 400 g each,
   drained
salt
fresh coriander to garnish

Preparation time: 15 minutes
Cooking time: 25–35 minutes

Each serving provides   Ⓥ
kcal 290, **protein** 13 g, **fat** 7 g (of which
saturated fat 1 g), **carbohydrate** 47 g (of
which sugars 22 g), **fibre** 12 g

✓✓	C
✓	B₁, B₆, folate, niacin, copper, iron, zinc

1 First, prepare the fruit. Peel the pineapple and cut out the core. Cut a few fine sticks of pineapple for the garnish and chop the rest into bite-sized chunks. Core the apples; cut half of one apple into thin wedges for the garnish and cut the remainder into dice. Put the fruit for the garnish in a bowl, sprinkle with the lemon juice and toss to coat. Cover with cling film and set aside.

2 Heat the oil in a saucepan and cook the onions with the garlic over a moderately high heat until they are lightly browned and softened. Add the diced apples and continue to cook, stirring frequently, until the dice are brown in places. Add the chunks of pineapple and cook for a few more minutes, stirring. Add the tomatoes and chilli powder or Tabasco and continue to cook for 10–15 minutes or until the mixture is sauce-like in consistency.

3 Add the beans to the fruit mixture in the pan and stir well. Continue to cook over a low heat for 5–10 minutes to mix and mingle the flavours.

4 Season to taste with salt. Garnish the beans and fruit with the reserved pineapple sticks and apple wedges and leaves of fresh coriander, and serve hot. For a Mexican-style presentation, accompany with flour tortillas plus a raw vegetable salad.

Plus points

● Tomatoes are well known as a good source of the antioxidants beta-carotene and vitamin C. But new research shows that the lycopene contained in tomatoes is even more important in the prevention of cancer, and is enhanced by cooking.

● Pulses contain both soluble and insoluble fibre. Insoluble fibre provides roughage, lessening the risk of bowel cancer, while soluble fibre has been connected with lowering cholesterol levels in the blood, thus reducing the risk of heart disease and stroke.

Another idea

● A similar Mexican dish is *lentejas costenas con frutas*, or lentils with fruit. Instead of the borlotti beans, cook 150 g (5½ oz) brown-green lentils in 700 ml (1¼ pints) of water with 2 bay leaves for about 30 minutes or until tender, then drain. Add the lentils to the fruit mixture at step 3. This mixture can be seasoned with cayenne pepper or Tabasco sauce instead of chilli powder; add with the salt.

Pears grilled with pecorino

Many cuisines have long traditions of combining fruit with cheese. This recipe stems from the Tuscan combination of juicy pears with salty ewe's milk pecorino. With some of the cheese melted over the pears and the rest combined with cool grapes and salad leaves, this makes a stylish first course, or light main dish for 2.

Serves 4

55 g (2 oz) pecorino cheese
1 bunch of watercress, about 55 g (2 oz),
    leaves removed from stalks
115 g (4 oz) rocket leaves
55 g (2 oz) seedless green grapes, halved
2 dessert pears
Balsamic vinaigrette
2 tbsp extra virgin olive oil
1 tbsp best-quality balsamic vinegar
½ tsp Dijon mustard
pinch of caster sugar
salt and pepper

Preparation time: 15 minutes
Cooking time: about 2 minutes

Each serving provides   Ⓥ
kcal 130, **protein** 4 g, **fat** 9 g (of which
saturated fat 3 g), **carbohydrate** 9 g (of which
sugars 9 g), **fibre** 2 g

✓✓	C
✓	A, B$_{12}$, folate, calcium

---

1 First make the dressing. Put the olive oil, balsamic vinegar, mustard, sugar, and salt and pepper to taste into a small screw-top jar. Screw on the lid and shake all the ingredients together until well blended. Keep the dressing in the fridge until required.

2 Preheat the grill to high. Place a strip of cooking foil on a baking tray and set aside.

3 Using a vegetable peeler, peel the pecorino cheese into fine shavings. Reserve half of these and finely chop the remainder. Put the watercress, rocket leaves and grapes into a salad bowl and toss together.

4 Peel, halve and core the pears. Arrange the pear halves, cut sides down, on the foil strip. Top the pears with the shavings of cheese, slightly overlapping them. Place under the grill, about 15 cm (6 in) from the heat, and grill for 2 minutes or until the cheese just starts to bubble and turn golden.

5 Meanwhile, shake the dressing, pour it over the salad and toss to coat the leaves. Add the chopped pecorino. Divide the salad equally among 4 plates.

6 Using a fish slice, carefully transfer one pear half to each plate, placing it on top of the bed of dressed salad. Serve at once.

Some more ideas
● Use diced kiwi fruit instead of grapes.
● Parmesan cheese, another Italian firm cheese, is suitable for this recipe and it has less fat.
● If you are in a hurry, just chop the pears and toss them in the salad with all the cheese.
● Substitute baby spinach leaves for the rocket.
● Grill the pear halves cut side up, then sprinkle a blue cheese, such as Shropshire blue, into the cavities and grill until it melts.
● A creamy goat's cheese could be used in a fruit and cheese salad instead of high-fat pecorino. Goat's cheese has a natural affinity with fresh raspberries, so for a stylish first course, omit the pears and pecorino cheese from the recipe above and replace the balsamic vinegar in the vinaigrette with raspberry vinegar. Toss 200 g (7 oz) raspberries with the salad. Toast 8 thin slices of baguette on one side under the grill, then turn over and top with slices of goat's cheese. Grill until the cheese is bubbling, then transfer 2 slices to each plate. Dress the salad and arrange next to the cheese-topped toasts.

Plus points
● This salad is a useful source of calcium, needed for healthy bones and teeth. The pecorino cheese, watercress and rocket all provide this vital mineral.

Fast Fruit Desserts

Mouthwatering sweets in 30 minutes or less

FRESH FRUIT – a peach or a bowl of berries – is the quickest of quick puddings, but, with just a little time and a few flavourful additions, fruit can easily be turned into something more special. Try mixing puréed apricots with whisked egg whites, then bake to a fluffy soufflé, or wrap plums in paper parcels with spices and honey. Comfort yourself with 'eggy bread' topped with glazed bananas, or a fruity sweet risotto. Enjoy peach and blackberry 'pizzas', or a fresh plum sauce for frozen yogurt or ice-cream. Relish a deliciously rich, lower-fat berry fool. None of these puddings will take you more than 30 minutes, and they're all good for you, too!

Flambéed Asian pears with orange

A delicious yet simple dessert, this is ready in just 25 minutes. Flaming the brandy burns off the alcohol, leaving a wonderful flavour which perfectly complements the oranges and pears. Even after cooking, Asian pears retain their crunchy texture, making a pleasant change from the more common dessert pears.

Serves 4

2 Asian pears
juice of ½ lemon
3 oranges
30 g (1 oz) butter
3 tbsp soft brown sugar
3 tbsp brandy
2 tbsp coarsely chopped pistachios
sprigs of fresh lemon balm to decorate

Preparation time: 15 minutes
Cooking time: 10 minutes

1 Peel, quarter and core the Asian pears. Cut them into slices and sprinkle with the lemon juice to prevent them from turning brown.

2 Peel the oranges, removing all the white pith. Cut them across into neat slices.

3 Melt the butter in a frying pan. Add the sugar and stir until dissolved. Add the pear slices and cook gently for about 3 minutes on each side or until they are just tender but still quite firm. Add the orange slices for the last minute of cooking, turning them to coat well with the juices in the pan.

4 Using a draining spoon, remove the pears and oranges to a shallow serving dish and keep warm. Boil the juices remaining in the pan to reduce a little, then pour over the fruit. Pour the brandy into the frying pan, heat it and set alight. Pour over the fruit.

5 Serve on warmed plates, sprinkled with the pistachios and decorated with lemon balm.

Some more ideas

• Use sliced dessert pears instead of Asian pears. They will need only about 2 minutes cooking on each side to make them tender.

• Use Poire Williams liqueur or Cointreau instead of brandy.

• Replace the pears with apples, cut in rings. Cox's are particularly good prepared this way. Flambé with Calvados and sprinkle with chopped toasted hazelnuts.

Plus points

• Oranges are justly famous for their vitamin C content (54 mg per 100 g/3½ oz). This is one of the 'water-soluble' vitamins, which cannot be stored by the body, so it is essential that fruit and vegetables containing vitamin C are eaten every day. As scientists have increasingly recognised, this vitamin helps to prevent a number of degenerative diseases such as heart disease and cancer, through its powerful antioxidant activity.

Each serving provides   Ⓥ
kcal 200, **protein** 3 g, **fat** 9 g (of which saturated fat 4 g), **carbohydrate** 24 g (of which sugars 23 g), **fibre** 3 g

✓✓	C
✓	E, folate

Grilled fruit brochettes

Cooking fruit on skewers, just long enough to heat the fruit through and slightly caramelise its sugars, is an easy and fun way of enjoying fresh fruit. If you are having a barbecue, cook the fruit brochettes over the charcoal fire – but take care not to char the fruit or leave it too long in the smoke.

Serves 4
½ medium-sized ripe pineapple
2 just ripe, firm bananas
2 ripe but firm pears
4 ripe but firm fresh figs
2 ripe but firm peaches
juice of 1 lemon
4 tsp sugar
cape gooseberries to decorate
Raspberry-orange coulis
225 g (8 oz) raspberries
grated zest and juice of ½ orange
1½ tbsp sugar, or to taste

Preparation time: 20 minutes
Cooking time: 6–7 minutes

1 Soak 8 bamboo skewers in cold water for 20 minutes.

2 Meanwhile, make the coulis. Purée the raspberries with the orange zest and juice and the sugar in a blender or food processor. If you like, sieve the purée to remove the raspberry pips. Taste the coulis and add a little more sugar, if necessary. Set aside.

3 Preheat the grill. Prepare the pineapple, bananas, pears, figs and peaches, peeling as necessary and cutting into attractive bite-sized pieces. Thread the fruit onto the soaked skewers, alternating them to make a colourful arrangement.

4 Sprinkle the kebabs with half of the lemon juice and sugar. Grill them for 3–4 minutes or until lightly tinged with brown, then turn over, sprinkle with the remaining lemon juice and sugar and grill for a further 3 minutes or until the second side is lightly browned and caramelised a little.

5 While the kebabs are being grilled, pull back the papery skins on the cape gooseberries to form a star-like flower round the fruit.

6 Place 2 fruit kebabs on each plate, drizzle round the coulis, decorate with cape gooseberries and serve hot.

Plus points
● This delicious recipe provides useful amounts of important antioxidant vitamins – plenty of vitamin C from the raspberries and the orange and lemon juices, and vitamin A converted from the beta-carotene in the peaches. As the fruit is heated for only a very short time, most of the vitamin C is retained.
● There is plenty of dietary fibre – both soluble and insoluble – in this array of fruit, and this is essential to keep the digestive tract healthy. Insoluble fibre provides bulk and prevents constipation. The soluble fibre found in fruit can be fermented by bacteria in the gut, producing substances that help to protect against bowel cancer.

Some more ideas
● Use nectarines instead of peaches.
● Use apples when peaches are not in season.
● Serve the fruit kebabs raw, just the fresh fruit skewers resting in a pool of the coulis.

Each serving provides Ⓥ
kcal 220, **protein** 3 g, **fat** 1 g (of which saturated fat 0.2 g), **carbohydrate** 54 g (of which sugars 53 g), **fibre** 7 g

✓✓✓ C

✓ B$_1$, niacin, copper, potassium

Hot apricot soufflés

Keep cans of apricots or other fruit packed in fruit juice in your storecupboard and you will be able to make these impressive-looking, light and fluffy dessert soufflés in a matter of minutes. These simple desserts do not contain the large amounts of sugar and eggs found in most sweet soufflé recipes.

Serves 4

1½ tsp ground almonds or caster sugar

1 can apricot halves in natural juice, about 400 g, well drained

2 eggs, separated

2 tbsp double cream

1 tbsp caster sugar

½ tsp pure vanilla extract

½ tsp lemon juice

½ tsp cream of tartar

To finish

icing sugar

cocoa powder (optional)

Preparation time: about 10 minutes

Cooking time: 15 minutes

Each serving provides ⓥ

kcal 155, **protein** 5 g, **fat** 9 g (of which saturated fat 4 g), **carbohydrate** 13 g (of which sugars 13 g), **fibre** 1 g

✓✓	B₁₂, C
✓	A, E

1 Preheat the oven to 200°C (400°F, gas mark 6) and place a baking tray inside to heat. Lightly butter four 175 ml (6 fl oz) ramekins and dust the sides with the ground almonds or caster sugar, shaking out the excess.

2 Put the apricot halves, egg yolks, cream, sugar, vanilla extract and lemon juice in a food processor or blender and process until smooth.

3 Place the egg whites in a clean bowl and whisk until soft peaks form. Sift over the cream of tartar and continue whisking until stiff peaks form. Spoon the apricot mixture over the egg whites and use a large metal spoon to fold together, taking care not to overmix and deflate the egg whites.

4 Divide the apricot mixture among the prepared ramekins. Use a round-bladed knife to mark a circle in the centre of each soufflé; this helps the tops to rise evenly.

5 Place the ramekins on the heated baking sheet and bake in the centre of the oven for 15 minutes or until the soufflés are well risen and golden brown on top. Immediately dust with icing sugar, or a mixture of icing sugar and cocoa powder, sifted through a sieve, and serve at once.

Plus points

● Using fruit canned in natural juice, rather than in syrup, cuts the sugar and thus the amount of calories.

● Eggs are a first-class source of protein – an essential nutrient for good health and well-being.

Some more ideas

● For double-fruit soufflés, drain a second can of apricot halves and finely chop the fruit. Flavour the apricots with a little very finely chopped preserved stem ginger or ground mixed spice. Prepare 6 ramekins, instead of 4. Make the soufflé mixture as above. Divide the chopped fruit among the ramekins, then top with the soufflé mixture and bake.

● Substitute pears canned in natural juice and add a pinch of ground cardamom to the mixture. Other fruits to try are blackcurrants and peaches.

● Save the fruit juice to add to a fruit salad or make into a fruit drink.

Saffron and vanilla grilled fruit

This warm medley of luscious fruit is elegantly spiced with a marinade of saffron and vanilla. It is delicious on its own for a virtually no-fat dessert, or can be topped with a fruity sorbet, vanilla frozen yogurt or ice-cream.

Serves 4

small pinch of saffron threads

1 tsp pure vanilla extract

1 tbsp honey

2 tbsp Marsala wine or sweet sherry

juice of 1 orange

2 bananas

100 g (3½ oz) black grapes

1 papaya

2 kiwi fruit

1 Ugli fruit

To serve (optional)

4 scoops frozen yogurt, ice-cream or
   sorbet

Preparation time: 15 minutes, plus 1 hour
   optional marinating

Cooking time: 5 minutes

Each serving (fruit alone) provides Ⓥ

kcal 130, protein 2 g, fat 0.5 g, carbohydrate
30 g (of which sugars 26 g), fibre 2 g

✓✓✓ C

✓   folate, potassium

---

1 Heat a small dry pan over a high heat, add the saffron threads and toast for 30 seconds or until fragrant. Place the toasted saffron in a mortar and crush it with a pestle until fine. Add 4 tbsp hot water to the saffron and stir.

2 Transfer the saffron liquid to a mixing bowl and stir in the vanilla extract, honey, Marsala or sherry and orange juice.

3 Add the fruit to the saffron and vanilla marinade as you prepare it. Peel the bananas and cut them into bite-sized chunks. Pick the grapes from their stalks and add them whole to the marinade. Peel the papaya, remove the seeds and cut into bite-sized chunks. Peel the kiwi fruit and quarter it lengthways. Peel the Ugli fruit, removing all the white pith, and cut out the segments from between the membranes. Stir the fruit in the marinade. If time permits, cover the bowl tightly with cling film and leave the fruit to marinate for 1 hour before cooking.

4 Preheat the grill. Pour the fruit and marinade into a shallow ovenproof dish. Spread out the fruit in an even layer. Grill for 5 minutes or until all the fruit is heated through. Serve the fruit warm, topping each serving with a scoop of frozen yogurt, ice-cream or sorbet, if you like.

Plus points

• Long cooking will destroy a lot of the vitamin C in fruit, but most will survive the short cooking time in this recipe. Fibre and minerals are not affected by heat. The bananas, kiwi fruit and citrus fruit here provide potassium, which keeps body fluids in balance and blood pressure down.

• Papaya is a useful source of vitamin A (from the beta-carotene it contains), which is needed for good vision. This tropical fruit plays a vital role in preventing blindness in many parts of the world where those foods that provide most vitamin A in the UK (full-fat milk, cheese, butter and egg yolks) are not part of the average diet.

Some more ideas

• Make a tropical version of this dish by replacing the grapes with 2 thick slices of fresh pineapple, cut into chunks, and 3–4 fresh ripe apricots, halved and stoned. To make the tropical marinade, omit the toasted saffron and hot water mixture and simply stir 1 tsp ground cinnamon with the vanilla extract and honey; use rum instead of Marsala or sherry, and the juice of 2 limes instead of orange juice.

• Stone fruit, such as peaches, apricots and cherries, can be added to this warm fruit salad, if liked, but avoid using melons.

• Use 2 oranges instead of the Ugli fruit.

Plums en papillote with honey

En papillote *is a method of cooking food in the oven in parcels of paper, thus sealing in all the delicious juices. It is important to use baking parchment for the parcels as its coating is more moistureproof than greaseproof paper. When the parcels are opened for serving, a wonderful spicy perfume is released.*

Serves 4

8 large dessert plums, stoned and thickly sliced

30 g (1 oz) unsalted butter

2 cinnamon sticks, halved

8 whole cloves

4 tbsp acacia honey, or another clear variety

1 large orange

To serve

4 scoops vanilla frozen yogurt or ice-cream

3 tbsp coarsely chopped pecans

extra honey for drizzling (optional)

Preparation time: 10 minutes

Cooking time: 20 minutes

1 Preheat the oven to 200°C (400°F, gas mark 6).

2 Take 4 large squares of baking parchment and in the centre of each put a quarter of the plum slices and butter, a piece of cinnamon stick and 2 whole cloves. Drizzle 1 tbsp of honey over each portion of plums.

3 Use a citrus zester to take fine shreds of zest from the orange, or thinly pare off the zest with a vegetable peeler and then cut it into fine shreds. Squeeze the juice from the orange. Add a quarter of the orange zest and juice to each portion of plums, sprinkling the zest and juice over the fruit evenly.

4 For each parcel, bring two opposite sides of the paper together over the fruit filling and fold two or three times. Fold over the other ends twice, then tuck them underneath, to make a neatly sealed parcel.

5 Place the parcels on a baking tray and bake for 20 minutes. The paper parcels will puff a little and brown slightly, and the fruit mixture inside will be bubbling hot.

6 Place the parcels on individual serving plates, carefully open up each one and top with a scoop of frozen yogurt or ice-cream. Sprinkle with the pecans and drizzle with extra honey, if you like. Serve immediately.

Some more ideas

• For pineapple and banana *en papillote*, replace the plums and spices with 1 small ripe pineapple, peeled, cored and chopped, and 4 bananas, thickly sliced. Add 2 star anise to each parcel, then drizzle with the honey and orange zest and juice.

• Maple syrup makes a toffee-flavoured alternative to honey.

• You can use foil for the parcels rather than baking parchment, but transfer the fruit compote to bowls for serving.

Plus points

• Plums contain a useful amount of vitamin E, an important antioxidant that helps to protect against degenerative diseases associated with ageing.

• Pecans, like other nuts, are rich in fat (70 g per 100 g/3½ oz), but little of this is saturated. They also provide generous amounts of vitamin E.

• Yogurt, along with other dairy products, is a valuable source of calcium. This mineral is essential for the structure of bones and teeth, which contain 99% of all calcium in the body. But calcium is also important in a number of other vital processes, including blood clotting and the proper functioning of muscles and nerves.

Each serving provides ⓥ

kcal 270, **protein** 3 g, **fat** 14 g (of which saturated fat 5 g), **carbohydrate** 35 g (of which sugars 34 g), **fibre** 3 g

✓✓	C, E
✓	A, calcium, copper, potassium

fast fruit desserts

Glazed banana pain perdu

Based on two nursery favourites – 'eggy bread' and comforting banana sandwiches – this more glamorous version is bound to become a new favourite with family and friends. Other fruit, such as strawberries and pears, can be used to ring the changes, with brioche slices or other bread as the base.

Serves 4

2 eggs

4 tbsp semi-skimmed milk

1 tsp honey

large pinch of ground cinnamon

8 small slices Granary bread

2 tsp sunflower oil

2 large bananas

To glaze

3 tbsp icing sugar

pinch of ground cinnamon

To decorate

icing sugar

fresh mint leaves

Preparation time: 5 minutes

Cooking time: 5–7 minutes

1 Preheat the grill. In a shallow dish, gently whisk together the eggs, milk, honey and cinnamon.

2 Trim the top and bottom crusts off the bread, if very crusty.

3 Heat a non-stick frying pan and brush with a little of the oil. Quickly dip each piece of bread in the egg mixture to moisten on both sides, then put it into the hot pan. Cook for 1–2 minutes or until pale golden brown on both sides. You may need to cook the bread slices in two batches, brushing the pan with a little more oil when necessary. As the bread is done, transfer to the grill pan.

4 Peel the bananas and cut into thin diagonal slices, arranging them on the bread slices to cover generously. Mix the icing sugar with the cinnamon and sprinkle over the bananas. Place under the grill to melt the sugar and glaze the fruit.

5 Sprinkle a little icing sugar over a few mint leaves and use to decorate the pain perdu. Serve immediately.

Some more ideas

• Try slices of sweet brioche loaf, topped with sliced strawberries spiced with a sprinkling of ground ginger.

• Spiced fruit breads make delicious pain perdu. Top with peach or pear slices spiced with a little freshly grated nutmeg.

• Leftover day-old bread is the best to use for this recipe as it absorbs the egg slightly better than very fresh, moist bread.

Plus points

• Bread has suffered in the past from a false reputation of being 'fattening' and its positive features have been overlooked. Even white bread provides some dietary fibre, and by law it is fortified with vitamins and minerals, including calcium and B_1.

• Eggs provide high-quality protein as well as iron and the fat-soluble vitamins A and E. Although eggs contain cholesterol, the hazards of eating eggs have often been exaggerated. Normally, dietary cholesterol has little effect on blood cholesterol levels.

Each serving provides ⒱

kcal 300, **protein** 10 g, **fat** 7 g (of which saturated fat 2 g), **carbohydrate** 53 g (of which sugars 26 g), **fibre** 3 g

✓✓✓	B_{12}
✓✓	E, folate, niacin
✓	B_1, B_2, B_6, calcium, copper, zinc

fast fruit desserts

104

105

Peach and blackberry filo pizzas

These simple, attractive tarts have a crisp filo pastry base and a luscious fresh fruit topping. Filo pastry is made with very little fat, and most of it you add yourself when you brush the sheets sparingly with butter.

Serves 4

10 sheets filo pastry, about 30 x 20 cm
   (12 x 8 in) each, thawed if frozen
30 g (1 oz) unsalted butter, melted
2 tsp ground almonds or hazelnuts
4 peaches, about 115 g (4 oz) each
150 g (5½ oz) blackberries
2 tbsp vanilla caster sugar
To serve (optional)
Greek-style yogurt

Preparation time: 15 minutes
Cooking time: 15 minutes

1 Preheat the oven to 200°C (400°F, gas mark 6).

2 Place a sheet of filo on the work surface and brush very lightly all over with melted butter. Top with another sheet and brush with butter. Layer on 3 more filo sheets, brushing with butter each time, and finally brush the top surface. Using a saucer measuring about 13 cm (5½ in) as a guide, cut out 2 discs from the layered filo. Transfer to a baking tray. Repeat with the remaining filo pastry and butter to make 4 layered discs in total.

3 Sprinkle each filo disc with ½ tsp of the ground almonds or hazelnuts, then set aside.

4 Cut the peaches in half, twist apart and remove the stones. Slice the peaches thinly. Place the peach slices on the filo pastry discs, arranging them so they leave a little of the pastry edge uncovered all round. Divide the blackberries among the pizzas. Sprinkle 1½ tsp sugar over each pizza.

5 Bake for 15 minutes or until the pastry is golden brown and the peaches are very tender and lightly caramelised. Transfer to individual plates and serve at once, with Greek-style yogurt, if liked. These filo pizzas are best served within 15 minutes of coming out of the oven as the pastry will quickly lose its crispness.

Plus points
● Even though the filo pastry is brushed with butter, the quantity used here is small compared to that normally used in similar filo preparations, and the total fat content is lower than tarts made with shortcrust.
● Peaches are a good source of carbohydrate, with virtually no fat. Fresh peaches are also low in calories, with an average peach containing only 30 kcal.
● Blackberries provide lots of vitamins C and E, as well as being rich in bioflavonoids that work with vitamin C as antioxidants to boost immunity.

Each serving (pizza alone) provides Ⓥ
kcal 200, **protein** 3 g, **fat** 9 g (of which saturated fat 3 g), **carbohydrate** 27 g (of which sugars 18 g), **fibre** 3 g

✓✓ C, E

Some more ideas

- Use raspberries instead of blackberries, and nectarines instead of peaches.
- To make pear pizzas, replace the peaches and blackberries with 2 dessert pears, peeled, cored and sliced. Toss the slices with 1 tsp ground coriander before arranging on the filo discs and baking.
- For even quicker preparation, use peeled and sliced fruit preserved in alcohol. Particularly delicious are well-drained peaches in brandy, with fresh blackberries or raspberries.
- For a more conventional tart shape, trim the filo discs to 11 cm (4½ in) and press them into shallow, non-stick Yorkshire pudding tins. Bake as above, but watch that the edges do not burn.
- Vanilla-flavoured caster sugar, sold in supermarkets and delicatessens, adds extra flavour. If you can't find any, make your own by submerging a split vanilla pod in a bag of caster sugar for at least a week. Alternatively, toss the peach slices with ground cinnamon or ground mixed spice and then use plain caster sugar for the glaze.
- When berries are out of season, use well-drained preserved stem ginger, finely chopped – 2–3 tsp for each filo pizza.

Cranberry and banana rice pudding

This could really be called a sweet risotto as it uses risotto rice. The starchy grains are ideal as they create a creamy-textured milk pudding in less than 20 minutes. Rather than sweetening it with lots of sugar, it is simmered with dried bananas and cranberries, both of which add natural sweetness.

Serves 4

1 litre (1¾ pints) semi-skimmed milk
140 g (5 oz) risotto rice
1 vanilla pod, split open in half
30 g (1 oz) light muscovado sugar
55 g (2 oz) dried cranberries
55 g (2 oz) small dried bananas, sliced
scented geranium leaves to decorate
   (optional)
To serve
berry coulis (see page 25) or other fruit
   coulis

Preparation time: 5 minutes
Cooking time: 15–20 minutes

1 Pour the milk into a heavy-based saucepan and add the rice, vanilla pod, sugar, cranberries and bananas. Stir to mix. Bring to the boil over a moderate heat, stirring constantly, then turn the heat down so the mixture is gently simmering. Cook, stirring frequently, for 15 minutes or until the pudding has a creamy consistency and the rice is tender.

2 Remove the vanilla pod from the pudding. Spoon the rice pudding into the centre of large flat soup plates. Drizzle with a few spoonfuls of the coulis and decorate with scented geranium leaves, if liked. Serve the remainder of the coulis separately.

Some more ideas

• You can make the rice pudding ahead of time to serve later, but you will need to add extra milk when reheating to return the pudding to its creamy consistency.

• For a creamy cinnamon and sultana rice pudding, replace the dried cranberries and banana with 75 g (2½ oz) sultanas and use a cinnamon stick instead of the vanilla pod. Serve with a tangy apricot coulis made by puréeing a well-drained can of apricot halves in apple and apricot juice, about 410 g, adding enough of the juice to make a smooth sauce.

Plus points

• Milk is one of our most nourishing foods. It is rich in calcium, which is essential for healthy teeth and bones, and is also a good source of protein.

• Unless catering for children under the age of 2, who always require full-fat milk, it is a good idea for everyone following a healthy diet to switch to semi-skimmed milk to reduce their intake of saturated fats.

• Cranberries, bananas and rice all boost the carbohydrate content of this dessert, and add a variety of vitamins as well.

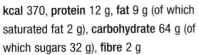

Each serving (with coulis) provides
kcal 370, **protein** 12 g, **fat** 9 g (of which saturated fat 2 g), **carbohydrate** 64 g (of which sugars 32 g), **fibre** 2 g

✓✓✓	C
✓✓	calcium, potassium
✓	B_{12}

fast fruit desserts

Summer fruit fool

A quick pudding to rustle up at a moment's notice, this can be made with almost any fruit in season. The usual whipped double cream in fruit fool is replaced here with a mixture of low-fat yogurt and whipping cream, yet despite the fat content being reduced, this is still a wonderfully rich and creamy dessert.

Serves 4

300 g (10½ oz) mixed soft fruit, such as
    raspberries, blackberries, blueberries or
    currants
55 g (2 oz) caster sugar
150 ml (5 fl oz) whipping cream
grated zest of ½ orange
150 g (5½ oz) plain low-fat bio yogurt
finely shredded orange zest to decorate
    (optional)

Preparation time: 20 minutes, plus cooling
    and chilling

1 Reserve about 55 g (2 oz) of the mixed fruit for decoration. Put the remaining mixed fruit in a saucepan with 2 tbsp water. Bring just to the boil, then reduce the heat and cook gently for 5 minutes or until soft and very juicy. Stir in the sugar.

2 Remove from the heat and leave to cool slightly. Pour into a food processor or blender and purée. Press the purée through a sieve to remove all the pips. Alternatively, just press the fruit through a sieve to purée it. Set aside to cool completely.

3 Whip the cream with the grated orange zest until thick. Add the yogurt and lightly whip into the cream, then mix in the cooled fruit purée.

4 Spoon into dessert dishes or goblets. Chill well before serving, decorated with the reserved berries and orange zest, if using.

Some more ideas

• For gooseberry fool, replace the soft fruit with 450 g (1 lb) gooseberries (don't reserve any for decoration) and increase the caster sugar to 115 g (4 oz). Cook the gooseberries for about 15 minutes or until softened. This gooseberry fool will serve 6.

• For a strawberry fool, slice 225 g (8 oz) ripe strawberries, reserving 4 whole ones for decoration, and sprinkle with the sugar. Leave for 30 minutes or until the juices are running from the fruit, then purée. Add to the cream and yogurt mixture. Serve decorated with the reserved strawberries, quartered or sliced.

• For a guava fool, roughly chop 225 g (8 oz) ripe guavas, with their skins, and purée in a food processor or blender with 45 g (1½ oz) sugar. Press through a sieve, then taste the purée and add a little more sugar if it isn't sweet enough. Fold into the cream and yogurt mixture with 1 tbsp orange liqueur. Guava is an excellent source of vitamin C.

Each serving provides Ⓥ
kcal 230, **protein** 3 g, **fat** 15 g (of which saturated fat 9 g), **carbohydrate** 22 g (of which sugars 22 g), **fibre** 2 g

✓✓✓	C
✓✓	A
✓	B₂, calcium

Plus points

• Yogurt is a good source of calcium. Throughout life, but particularly during adolescence and pregnancy, it is important for women to get enough calcium to keep bones healthy and prevent osteoporosis later.
• The mixed soft fruit are all rich in the antioxidant vitamin C, and their natural acidity helps to prevent the loss of this vitamin during the cooking. To retain as much vitamin C as possible, the sugar is added after the fruit is softened.

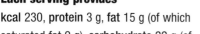

fast fruit desserts

Hot plum sauce

The rich colour of this sauce is stunning, and with its tartness and temperature, it provides a good contrast to vanilla frozen yogurt or ice-cream, or to any plain pudding or cake. A home-made fruit sauce such as this is a good alternative to chocolate, butterscotch or other sweet sauces (also see the coulis recipes on page 25).

Serves 4

450 g (1 lb) ripe dessert plums

150 ml (5 fl oz) orange juice

large pinch of ground cinnamon

large pinch of ground cloves

1 tsp light soft brown sugar, or to taste

1 tsp brandy (optional)

To serve

vanilla frozen yogurt or ice-cream

Preparation time: 5–10 minutes

Cooking time: about 10 minutes

1 Cut the plums in half and remove the stones. Put the fruit in a saucepan and add the orange juice, cinnamon and cloves. Bring slowly to the boil, then reduce the heat and simmer gently for 10 minutes or until the fruit is very soft.

2 Press the fruit mixture through a sieve into a bowl. Add the sugar and stir to mix, then taste the sauce and add more sugar if necessary. Add the brandy, if using.

3 If necessary, return the sauce to a clean saucepan and reheat gently. Serve hot, poured over scoops of frozen yogurt or ice-cream.

Some more ideas

• Canned plums can be used instead of fresh. Drain 1 can of plums in syrup, about 565 g, and sieve the fruit. Follow the recipe from step 2, omitting the sugar.

• When damsons are in season, use them to make this sauce. You may need to sweeten with additional sugar as damsons are more sour than other plums.

• For a hot blackberry sauce, substitute blackberries for the plums and use apple juice instead of orange juice. Blackberries will need only 5 minutes of gentle simmering.

• For a very quick fruit sauce, thaw a 500 g bag of frozen summer fruit, sieve the fruit with the juice it yields, and serve hot or cold.

Plus points

• Plums provide dietary fibre, both the insoluble type, which plays a particularly important role in preventing constipation, and soluble fibre, which helps to protect against some forms of cancer.

• Plums contain little vitamin C compared to other fruit, but this is made up for here by the orange juice.

• Frozen yogurt or ice-cream are good ways of adding calcium to the diet of children and teenagers, who have especially high requirements for this mineral as they grow.

Each serving (sauce alone) provides Ⓥ

kcal 60, **protein** 1 g, **fat** 0 g, **carbohydrate** 15 g (of which sugars 15 g), **fibre** 2 g

✓✓   C

Good Puddings

Fruity desserts that all the family will love

EATING WELL BY BOOSTING FRUIT, vegetables and carbohydrate foods and cutting down on fat and sugar doesn't mean that you can't enjoy favourite puddings. Take advantage of fruit's natural sweetness and its myriad colours and textures to make irresistible yet healthy desserts. Add sweet-tart rhubarb to a rich crème brûlée, kumquats to a steamed pudding, or exotic fruit to a trifle. Try topping a cheesecake with mixed citrus segments, or a chocolate mousse cake with cherries. Or freeze abundant summer berries in an ice-cream, granita or frozen yogurt for a year-round treat. These fabulous fruity puddings will delight family and friends alike.

Cape gooseberry and apple crumble

Cape gooseberries, also known as physalis or Chinese lanterns, add a pleasing sharpness to apple crumble, while the fruit juice and dried blueberries bring natural sweetness. Rolled oats and chopped nuts give an appealing crunch to the crumble topping, which is made with less sugar than most recipes suggest.

Serves 6

Filling

1 kg (2¼ lb) dessert apples, such as Cox's or Braeburns

4 tbsp dried blueberries

4 tbsp orange juice

100 g (3½ oz) cape gooseberries, papery skins discarded

1 tbsp sugar

Crumble topping

125 g (4½ oz) plain flour

100 g (3½ oz) unsalted butter, diced

55 g (2 oz) caster sugar

50 g (1¾ oz) rolled oats

50 g (1¾ oz) hazelnuts or walnuts, chopped

grated zest of 1 orange

To serve

custard (see page 128)

Preparation time: 35 minutes

Cooking time: 20–25 minutes

1 Preheat the oven to 200°C (400°F, gas mark 6).

2 Peel the apples, cut them into thick wedges and remove the core. Place them in a saucepan with the blueberries and orange juice. Cover the pan and cook over a low heat for 10 minutes or until the apples start to soften and release their juices.

3 Add the whole cape gooseberries and sugar to the apples and stir. Transfer the fruit filling to a 1.5 litre (2¾ pint) deep baking dish.

4 In a mixing bowl, rub the flour and butter together until the mixture resembles fine breadcrumbs. Stir in the sugar, oats, hazelnuts or walnuts, and orange zest, then mix in about 1 tbsp water to give a very rough, crumbly mixture. Spread the crumble topping gently and evenly over the fruit. Do not press down.

5 Bake for 20–25 minutes or until the topping is golden brown and the fruit juice is bubbling up round the edges. Serve hot, with custard.

Plus points

● Oats are an excellent source of soluble fibre which helps to slow the absorption of carbohydrate (particularly glucose) into the bloodstream, resulting in a gentler rise and fall in blood sugar levels.

● Cape gooseberries contain beta-carotene and vitamin C as well as potassium.

Some more ideas

● Replace the cape gooseberries with 100 g (3½ oz) of chopped rhubarb. If liked, add a handful of strawberries too.

● 2 tbsp desiccated coconut can be mixed into the crumble topping.

● Use other dried fruits instead of blueberries – cranberries, raisins, sultanas and currants are all just as good.

Each serving (with custard) provides
kcal 458, **protein** 9 g, **fat** 23 g (of which saturated fat 11 g), **carbohydrate** 54 g (of which sugars 35 g), **fibre** 4 g

✓✓	E
✓	A, B₁, B₆, C

good puddings

116

Rhubarb and saffron crème brûlée

A tart compote of rhubarb makes a nice contrast to the rich custard here. While there is no way to completely streamline a crème brûlée, this special occasion treat is lightened by the fruit and has reduced amounts of cream and egg yolk, yet still retains its rich indulgent nature.

Serves 6

250 g (9 oz) rhubarb, chopped
juice of ½ orange
75 g (2½ oz) caster sugar, or to taste
250 ml (8½ fl oz) semi-skimmed milk
2 pinches of saffron threads
4 egg yolks
1 whole egg
3 tbsp double cream
4 tbsp demerara sugar

Preparation time: 20–25 minutes, plus cooling
    and at least 1 hour chilling
Cooking time: 25–35 minutes

Each serving provides   (V)

kcal 260, **protein** 5 g, **fat** 15 g (of which
saturated fat 8 g), **carbohydrate** 27 g (of
which sugars 27 g), **fibre** 1 g

✓✓	A, B₁₂
✓	B₂, E, calcium

1 Preheat the oven to 160°C (325°F, gas mark 3).

2 Put the rhubarb in a heavy-based saucepan with the orange juice and 3 tbsp of the caster sugar. Poach on a moderately low heat for 5–7 minutes or until the fruit is tender and juicy, but still keeps its shape. Leave to cool.

3 In another heavy saucepan, heat the milk with the remaining caster sugar and the saffron until bubbles appear round the edge. Beat together the egg yolks, whole egg and double cream. Slowly add the hot sweetened saffron milk to the egg mixture, stirring to mix.

4 Divide the rhubarb compote among 6 ramekin dishes, or spread over the bottom of a 1 litre (1¾ pint) shallow baking dish. To ladle the custard mixture over the fruit, place the base of the ladle on top of the fruit and turn it slowly to ease in the custard (if you pour it in, it will mix with the rhubarb and not form two separate layers).

5 Place the ramekins or baking dish in a large roasting tin. Pour boiling water into the tin to come about two-thirds up the sides of the dishes. Bake for 25 minutes for the ramekins or 35 minutes for the large dish, or until set.

6 Remove from the oven and leave to cool. Then chill for at least 1 hour or until quite cold.

7 Preheat the grill to high. Sprinkle the demerara sugar on top of the custard (2 tsp for each ramekin) and smooth it with your finger so that it forms an even layer. Grill close to the heat for just a moment or two until the sugar melts and bubbles, keeping a close watch on it so that it does not burn. Remove from the heat and allow to cool for a few minutes or until the sugar has hardened to a crust. Serve.

Some more ideas

● Replace the rhubarb with cooking gooseberries, topped and tailed, and the orange juice with 2 tbsp elderflower cordial.
● Instead of rhubarb, use 1 large cooking apple, peeled, cored and chopped, and 75 g (2½ oz) redcurrants.

Plus points

● Rhubarb is 94% water, and compared with soft fruit and citrus fruit contains very little vitamin C. However, it does provide vitamin A – the same amount as peaches – which is essential for healthy skin and good vision.
● Apart from providing protein, eggs also contain useful amounts of vitamins A, B₂, B₁₂, niacin and E.

Pear pancakes with chocolate sauce

Pears, almonds and chocolate make a delicious combination for a dessert to grace a special occasion. There is much less fat and sugar here than in similar recipes, but the rich, satisfying flavours have not been lost. The pancakes can be prepared in advance and frozen, if you like.

Serves 6

Pancake batter

115 g (4 oz) plain flour

1 egg

300 ml (10 fl oz) semi-skimmed milk

1 tbsp sunflower oil

Filling

115 g (4 oz) fromage frais

3 tbsp ground almonds

1 tbsp caster sugar

¼ tsp pure almond extract

5 ripe dessert pears

lemon juice

icing sugar

Chocolate sauce

115 g (4 oz) good plain chocolate (at least 70% cocoa solids)

2 tbsp caster sugar

Preparation time: 45 minutes, plus 30 minutes standing

Cooking time: 8–10 minutes

Each serving provides ⓥ

kcal 340, **protein** 8 g, **fat** 12 g (of which saturated fat 5 g), **carbohydrate** 52 g (of which sugars 38 g), **fibre** 3 g

✓✓	B₁₂, E
✓	B₁, B₂, C, niacin, calcium, iron

1 Preheat the oven to 200°C (400°F, gas mark 6). Place the batter ingredients in a food processor or blender and process until smooth. Alternatively, whisk together, adding the milk gradually. Pour into a jug and leave to stand for 30 minutes.

2 Heat a 15 cm (6 in) pancake or frying pan and add a few drops of oil. Pour in 1 tbsp of the batter and tilt the pan to coat the bottom evenly. Cook until the underside of the pancake is brown, then turn it over and cook for 10 seconds on the other side. Slide the pancake out onto a plate. Repeat to make 12 pancakes in all, turning each one out onto the plate, and separating with greaseproof paper. Set aside.

3 To make the filling, put the fromage frais, almonds, sugar and almond extract in a bowl and mix well. Peel, quarter and core the pears. Chop 4 into small dice; cut the remaining pear into neat slices and sprinkle with lemon juice to prevent discoloration.

4 Spoon 1 tbsp of the almond mixture onto a quarter area of each pancake and top with a spoonful of diced pear. Fold over each pancake into quarters to make a triangle, enclosing the filling. Place on a greased baking tray, sprinkle generously with icing sugar and bake for 8–10 minutes.

5 Meanwhile, make the chocolate sauce. Put the chocolate, sugar and 5 tbsp water in a saucepan and heat very gently until the chocolate has melted and the sugar dissolved. Simmer for 5 minutes or until smooth.

6 Serve the pancakes on individual plates, drizzled with the chocolate sauce. Arrange the reserved pear slices next to the pancakes and serve.

Some more ideas

• For raspberry pancakes, use 225 g (8 oz) raspberries instead of the pears. Serve with the chocolate sauce or with a berry coulis (see page 25) flavoured with kirsch.

• Replace the pears with 1 ripe mango, cut into small slices, and the pulp from 2 passion fruit. Instead of the chocolate sauce, use a mango coulis (see page 25). Varied this way, the dessert will be lower in fat and will provide more of those important antioxidant vitamins, A and C.

Plus points

• Milk and dairy products like fromage frais are good sources of calcium, protein and vitamin B₂. Full-fat products also contain vitamins A and D, but these are removed along with the fat in reduced-fat varieties.

Fruit and malt bread pudding

Aromatic malt loaf lends a healthy rich note to classic bread pudding, allowing you to reduce the fat without sacrificing any flavour as there is no need to spread the slices with butter. There is lots of dried fruit – dates, apricots, pears and apples – between the malt loaf layers, giving natural sweetness.

Serves 6

1 small malt loaf, about 225 g (8 oz)

55 g (2 oz) stoned dried dates, chopped

55 g (2 oz) ready-to-eat dried apricots, chopped

55 g (2 oz) ready-to-eat dried pears, chopped

55 g (2 oz) ready-to-eat dried apples, chopped

300 ml (10 fl oz) semi-skimmed milk

3 eggs

2 tbsp soft brown or demerara sugar

¼ tsp pure vanilla extract

caster or icing sugar to finish

Preparation time: 10 minutes, plus 30 minutes soaking

Cooking time: 40–50 minutes

1 Cut the malt loaf into 10 slices. Arrange half the slices in a 1.4 litre (2½ pint) ovenproof dish and sprinkle with the chopped dried fruit. Arrange the remaining slices of malt loaf on top.

2 In a small saucepan, heat the milk until bubbles form round the edge. Beat the eggs with the sugar and the vanilla extract in a bowl or jug. Pour the scalding milk over them, whisking constantly. Pour the custard mixture over the malt loaf and fruit and leave to soak for 30 minutes so that the malt loaf absorbs some of the liquid.

3 Preheat the oven to 160°C (325°F, gas mark 3).

4 Put the bread pudding in the oven and bake for 40–50 minutes or until set and golden.

5 Remove the pudding from the oven and leave to cool for 10 minutes or so. Sprinkle with a little caster or sifted icing sugar before serving.

Plus points

• This rich dessert, while being low in fat, provides useful fibre from the dried fruit (dates in particular) and protein from the eggs as well as plenty of carbohydrate.

• Eggs have received a 'bad press' in the last few years because of their cholesterol content, but they are an excellent source of many nutrients, including protein and iron, and they are low in fat.

Some more ideas

• Replace the dates with prunes. Substitute 4 tbsp of fresh orange juice for 4 tbsp of the milk and add the grated zest of 1 orange to the custard mixture, reducing the sugar to 1 tbsp.

• Fruited teabreads or raisin loaf can be used in place of the malt loaf. Alternatively, use day-old French bread, cut into small cubes, or stale white bread and add some sultanas or raisins.

Each serving provides

kcal 270, **protein** 10 g, **fat** 5 g (of which saturated fat 1 g), **carbohydrate** 50 g (of which sugars 38 g), **fibre** 3 g

✓✓	B$_{12}$
✓	B$_1$, B$_2$, E, niacin, calcium, iron, potassium

Baked almond-stuffed peaches

Baking fruit brings out its flavour wonderfully, and a stuffing is a simple way of making baked fruit special. Here peaches are filled with a mixture of dried apricots, almonds and amaretti biscuits. Many other fruits – nectarines, apples, pears or quinces – can be prepared in the same way, to ring the seasonal changes.

Serves 4

5 large ripe but firm peaches
10 ready-to-eat dried apricots, finely diced
6 amaretti biscuits, crumbled
2 tsp pure almond extract
1 tbsp brandy
1 egg white
55 g (2 oz) whole blanched almonds

Preparation time: 20 minutes
Cooking time: about 40 minutes

Each serving provides   ⓥ

kcal 200, **protein** 6 g, **fat** 9 g (of which saturated fat 1 g), **carbohydrate** 24 g (of which sugars 21 g), **fibre** 5 g

✓✓   C, E
✓   B₂, niacin, copper, potassium

1 Preheat the oven to 180°C (350°F, gas mark 4).

2 Cut the peaches in half and remove the stones. Arrange 8 of the halves, cut side up, in a shallow baking dish. Set aside. Finely dice the remaining 2 peach halves.

3 Combine the diced peach with the dried apricots, crumbled amaretti, almond extract, brandy and egg white. Stir to mix thoroughly.

4 Heat a small heavy ungreased frying pan and lightly toast the almonds, turning and tossing every so often, until they are lightly browned in spots. Remove and coarsely chop, in a food processor or by hand, to make a mixture of small chunks of nuts and ground nuts.

5 Add the chopped almonds to the fruit and amaretti mixture and mix well. Use to fill the hollows in the peach halves, heaping up the filling and pressing it gently together. Cover the baking dish with a tent of cooking foil.

6 Bake for 25–30 minutes, then remove the foil. Increase the oven temperature to 200°C (400°F, gas mark 6) and bake for a further 5–10 minutes or until the nutty topping is lightly browned. The peaches are best when warm, but they can be chilled before serving.

Some more ideas

● Nectarines can be used instead of peaches, with pistachios instead of almonds.

● Macaroons can be used instead of amaretti, but fewer according to size.

● For baked stuffed apples or pears, substitute sultanas for the diced dried apricots and add a few shakes of ground cinnamon to the filling. Allow 10 minutes longer baking time before removing the foil covering.

● Use quinces instead of peaches, allowing 15 minutes extra baking time.

● Use a mixture of peaches or nectarines, apples, pears and quinces, and make the filling from a mixture of these fruit. Allow 10–15 minutes extra baking time.

Plus points

● Peaches contain plenty of vitamin C (31 mg per 100 g/3½ oz) and this can help the body to absorb iron present in other foods – in this case from dried apricots. Iron deficiency anaemia is probably the most common deficiency disease in the UK, so every little bit helps. Dried apricots also provide vitamin A and plenty of potassium for regulating blood pressure.

● Almonds not only have a delicious and distinctive flavour, but also contain protein and plenty of vitamin E.

Cherry brandy clafoutis

Clafoutis is a classic French dessert in which fruit is baked in a sweetened batter. Both canned and fresh fruit are suitable, so this is an ideal dessert to make whatever is in season – even from storecupboard ingredients when time is short. Bake in individual flan dishes or one large dish.

Serves 4

2 cans stoned cherries in syrup, about
   425 g each
2 tbsp brandy
75 g (2½ oz) plain flour
55 g (2 oz) light muscovado sugar
250 ml (8½ fl oz) semi-skimmed milk
3 eggs
1 tsp pure vanilla extract
icing sugar to dust (optional)

Preparation time: 10 minutes
Cooking time: 20 minutes

1 Preheat the oven to 200°C (400°F, gas mark 6). Drain the cherries, then tip them onto kitchen paper and pat dry.

2 Divide the cherries equally among four 300 ml (10 fl oz) individual flan dishes, or other ovenproof dishes, spreading them in an even layer. Drizzle the brandy over the cherries. Set aside.

3 Sift the flour into a bowl and add the sugar. In a jug, beat the milk and eggs with the vanilla extract, then whisk into the flour mixture to make a smooth batter. Alternatively, combine the ingredients in a food processor and process until smooth.

4 Pour the batter slowly over the fruit. Bake for 20 minutes or until lightly set and pale golden. Dust with icing sugar, if you like, and serve warm.

Some more ideas

- Bake in one dish, if you prefer. Use a 25 cm (10 in) round china flan dish and bake for 20–25 minutes.
- Use fresh sweet cherries, stoned, rather than canned cherries.
- When fresh peaches are in season, replace the canned cherries with 4 ripe but firm peaches, peeled and sliced, and use peach schnapps instead of the brandy. Flavour the batter with 1 tsp mixed spice instead of vanilla, adding the spice to the flour. Peaches provide twice as much fibre, 10 times the amount of vitamin A and 30 times the amount of vitamin C per 100 g (3½ oz) as cherries.
- To reduce the fat a little more use skimmed milk rather than semi-skimmed.
- The tiny black seeds scraped from half a vanilla pod can be used as an alternative to the vanilla extract.

Plus points

- Cherries not only provide delicious flavour and fibre, but also vitamin B_1, essential for proper functioning of the nervous system, and a small amount of iron.
- If you were to use skimmed milk in the batter instead of semi-skimmed, to reduce the fat content, this would not affect the amount of calcium provided (calcium is particularly important for maintaining healthy bones). It's worth remembering, though, that reducing the fat will also reduce the amount of fat-soluble vitamins, so this is not recommended for children under the age of 2 (and possibly up to age 5, according to the child's general appetite and diet).

Each serving provides

kcal 380, **protein** 11 g, **fat** 6 g (of which saturated fat 2 g), **carbohydrate** 74 g (of which sugars 59 g), **fibre** 2 g

✓✓	B_{12}
✓	A, B_1, B_2, B_6, folate, niacin, calcium, iron

Steamed kumquat honey pudding

A pleasingly light yet traditional pudding for wintry days, this offers all the pleasure of a steamed pudding without the unhealthy saturated fat in suet. Layers of sliced kumquats add a deliciously tangy citrus flavour.

Serves 6

2 tbsp clear honey

150 g (5½ oz) fresh fine white breadcrumbs

100 g (3½ oz) demerara sugar

50 g (1¾ oz) self-raising flour

1 tsp baking powder

1 egg, beaten

2 tbsp semi-skimmed milk

30 g (1 oz) unsalted butter, at room
    temperature

225 g (8 oz) kumquats, sliced (with skin)

Custard

2 eggs

1 tbsp sugar

300 ml (10 fl oz) semi-skimmed milk

1 tsp pure vanilla extract

Preparation time: 15 minutes

Cooking time: 1¾ hours

Each serving provides Ⓥ

kcal 275, **protein** 6 g, **fat** 6 g (of which
saturated fat 3 g), **carbohydrate** 53 g (of
which sugars 28 g), **fibre** 2 g

✓✓ B₁₂, C, calcium

1 Put the honey in the bottom of a 900 ml (1½ pint) pudding basin and turn it so that the honey coats the bottom half of the basin. Set aside.

2 Put the breadcrumbs in a large mixing bowl. Stir in the sugar, flour and baking powder. Add the egg, milk and softened butter and mix together to form a stiff cake-like mixture.

3 Place a quarter of the pudding mixture in the bottom of the honey-lined pudding basin and arrange half of the kumquat slices on top. Add half the remaining mixture to the basin and top with the remaining kumquat slices. Finish with the last of the pudding mixture and press down lightly to smooth the surface.

4 Bring a steamer or deep pan of water to the boil. Cover the top of the pudding basin with cooking foil and secure it firmly with string tied round under the rim. Use some more string to make a handle. Place the pudding in the steamer. The water should come no more than halfway up the side of the basin. Cover and steam for 1¾ hours, topping up the water as necessary.

5 About 20 minutes before serving, make the custard. In a bowl, beat the eggs with the sugar and 3 tbsp of the milk. Put the rest of the milk in a heavy-based saucepan and heat until bubbles appear round the edge. Pour the hot milk onto the eggs, stirring, then strain the mixture back into the pan. Cook over a low heat, stirring constantly, until the custard thickens enough to coat the back of the spoon in a thin layer. Do not allow to boil. Stir in the vanilla extract.

6 When the pudding is cooked, carefully remove it from the steamer, lifting it by the string handle. Remove the foil covering, place a plate over the top of the basin and invert it. With a gentle shake, the pudding will fall out of the basin onto the plate. Serve hot, with the custard.

Another idea
- Use sliced oranges instead of kumquats.

Plus points
- Kumquats are not a true citrus fruit, but are closely related and so, not surprisingly, they are an excellent source of vitamin C. Although this vitamin is no longer believed to have a direct effect in preventing the common cold, it does help to maintain the immune system and may well modify the severity and duration of infections.
- Milk provides calcium and phosphorus – both important for strong bones and teeth – as well as protein and many B vitamins.

Raspberry queen of puddings

A great British favourite, this version of queen of puddings has a chocolate-flavoured base and is given the modern treatment with more fruit and less sugar and fat. Whenever there is leftover bread, turn it into breadcrumbs, by grating or whizzing in a food processor, then freeze until needed for a dish like this.

Serves 4

3 eggs

85 g (3 oz) caster sugar

300 ml (10 fl oz) semi-skimmed milk

2 tbsp cocoa powder

50 g (1¾ oz) fresh breadcrumbs

2 tbsp redcurrant jelly

150 g (5½ oz) raspberries, plus more to decorate

15 g (½ oz) flaked almonds

Preparation time: 15–20 minutes, plus 20 minutes standing

Cooking time: 35–45 minutes

Each serving provides Ⓥ

kcal 300, **protein** 11 g, **fat** 9 g (of which saturated fat 3 g), **carbohydrate** 46 g (of which sugars 36 g), **fibre** 2 g

✓✓ B₁₂, E

✓ B₂, C, niacin, calcium

1 Break 1 egg into a bowl. Separate the remaining 2 eggs, adding the yolks to the bowl with the whole egg, and placing the whites in a separate large bowl to set aside for the meringue.

2 Add 30 g (1 oz) of the sugar to the egg and yolks and whisk together until smoothly blended. Put the milk and cocoa in a saucepan and heat to boiling point. Whisk into the egg yolk mixture, then add the breadcrumbs.

3 Pour the mixture into 4 large individual soufflé dishes or into a shallow baking dish and set aside for 20 minutes so that the breadcrumbs can absorb some of the liquid. Preheat the oven to 160°C (325°F, gas mark 3).

4 Bake the pudding base, allowing 20 minutes for soufflé dishes or 30 minutes for a baking dish, until set.

5 Meanwhile, heat the redcurrant jelly gently in a saucepan until melted. Add the raspberries and crush lightly with the back of a spoon to mix them into the melted jelly. Heat gently for 2 minutes, then leave to cool.

6 Whisk the egg whites until stiff. Add the remaining 55 g (2 oz) of sugar and continue whisking until the meringue is glossy. Spoon the raspberry mixture over the pudding. Top with the meringue, piling it up and swirling into a peak. Sprinkle over the almonds.

7 Bake for about 15 minutes or until the meringue is pale golden brown. Serve immediately, decorated with a few extra raspberries.

Some more ideas

● Instead of raspberries and redcurrant jelly, use a mixture of chopped fresh apricots and apricot jam, or dried chopped apricots poached in a little apple juice until thick. Using dried apricots will boost the iron content.

● Omit the cocoa powder and flavour the custard with ½ tsp freshly grated nutmeg or five-spice powder.

● Top the meringue with chopped or flaked hazelnuts instead of almonds.

Plus points

● Raspberries not only provide plenty of vitamin C (32 mg per 100 g/3½ oz), but also contain the fat-soluble vitamin E. Vitamin E is an important antioxidant, also found in vegetables such as spinach and broccoli as well as in vegetable oils and nuts. The effects of vitamin E are enhanced by other antioxidants such as vitamin C and selenium, present here in the almonds.

● Using cocoa powder instead of chocolate to flavour the base reduces the fat and increases the amount of iron.

Pear and blueberry shortcrust

Instead of making traditional pastry and rolling it out to top a pie dish, this rich almond shortcrust is simply patted out or rolled directly on a baking sheet, to be cut into portions after baking and served with delicious poached fruit. This way you get to enjoy more fruit than can fit into a typical pie dish.

Serves 6

Almond shortcrust pastry

150 g (5½ oz) plain flour

75 g (2½ oz) unsalted butter

30 g (1 oz) caster sugar

2 tbsp ground almonds

few drops of pure almond extract

1 egg

Poached fruit

4 dessert pears

450 ml (15 fl oz) clear apple juice

150 g (5½ oz) blueberries

Preparation time: 20–25 minutes

Cooking time: 15–20 minutes

Each serving provides Ⓥ

kcal 310, **protein** 5 g, **fat** 14 g (of which saturated fat 7 g), **carbohydrate** 45 g (of which sugars 26 g), **fibre** 3 g

✓✓	E
✓	A, B₁, B₁₂, C

1 Preheat the oven to 200°C (400°F, gas mark 6). To make the pastry, put the flour, butter, sugar, ground almonds, almond extract and egg into a food processor. Process until the mixture is crumb-like and beginning to come together. Add a few drops of water if necessary. Alternatively, put all the ingredients in a bowl and mix together gently with your fingertips.

2 Transfer the crumbly dough to the centre of a baking tray lined with non-stick paper or a lining sheet. Pat out or roll out to form a circle about 20 cm (8 in) in diameter. Pinch the edges to scallop them and mark into 12 wedges. Prick all over with a fork.

3 Place the baking tray in the oven and bake the pastry for 15–20 minutes or until golden brown. Remove from the oven and cut through the marked lines to separate the wedges.

4 While the pastry is baking, peel the pears, cut each one into quarters and remove the core. Put the pears in a large saucepan. Pour over the apple juice and bring to the boil, then reduce the heat and simmer for 7–10 minutes or until the pears are almost tender. Add the blueberries and cook for a further 2 minutes or until the juices run and the pears take on the rich purple colour of the blueberries.

5 With a draining spoon, lift the pears and blueberries out onto a serving dish or individual serving plates. Raise the heat under the saucepan and boil to reduce the fruit juice to about 175 ml (6 fl oz). Pour over the fruit. Serve each portion of fruit with 2 pastry wedges.

Some more ideas

• Many other seasonal fruit can be given a similar treatment. Apples and blackberries are a traditional partnership.

• Use a compote of 340 g (12 oz) mixed dried fruit poached in apple or orange juice with chopped stem ginger; replace the almond extract in the pastry with 1 tsp ground ginger.

• Instead of making a pastry circle and marking it into wedges, press the pastry out into a square shape and mark into oblongs or triangles, or cut out small discs.

Plus points

• Blueberries, like all berries, are rich in vitamin C. They also provide beta-carotene. Both vitamin C and beta-carotene are very valuable antioxidants. They work together to fight harmful free radicals.

• When ripe, pears are deliciously sweet and full of natural sugars, so they can be used to add sweetness to desserts without adding refined sugar.

good puddings

Plum and marzipan pastries

Whole plums baked with toasted almonds and marzipan in light layers of flaky filo pastry makes a scrumptious dessert. Serve the pastries on their own or with a spoonful of Greek-style yogurt or reduced-fat crème fraîche.

Serves 4

5 large dessert plums, about 75 g (2½ oz) each

45 g (1½ oz) white marzipan, sliced into 4 portions

150 g (5½ oz) filo pastry, thawed if frozen

30 g (1 oz) unsalted butter, melted

4 tbsp toasted flaked almonds

1 tsp icing sugar mixed with a pinch of ground cinnamon

Preparation time: 15 minutes
Cooking time: 15–20 minutes

1 Preheat the oven to 180°C (350°F, gas mark 4). Halve the plums lengthways and ease out the stones. Cut one of the plums into slices and reserve for the decoration. Put a slice of marzipan in between the halves of each remaining plum and sandwich back together.

2 Cut the filo pastry into 8 squares, each measuring about 20 x 20 cm (8 x 8 in). Stack 2 squares of filo on top of each other, brushing lightly between the layers with melted butter and placing them so the corners are not directly aligned.

3 Pile 1 tbsp of the almonds in the centre of the pastry and place a marzipan-stuffed plum on top. Scrunch the pastry up round the plum to form an old-fashioned moneybag shape.

4 Repeat with the remaining pastry, almonds and plums to make 4 moneybags in all. Brush the pastries with any remaining butter.

5 Place on a non-stick baking tray. Bake for 15–20 minutes or until the pastry is crisp and golden. Transfer the pastries to serving plates. Dust with the icing sugar and cinnamon, decorate with the reserved plum slices, and serve.

Plus points

- The plums in this dessert are a delicious way to help get to the target of at least 5 portions of fruit and vegetables a day.
- Filo pastry makes a lower-fat alternative to puff and shortcrust pastries, as you can be very sparing with the butter added.
- Almonds and other nuts provide many of the nutrients usually obtained from meat. These include most of the B vitamins, phosphorus, iron, copper, potassium and, of course, protein.

Some more ideas

- For fig pastries, use ripe but still firm figs cut in half lengthways instead of the plums.
- To add an orange flavour, sprinkle the pastry with the finely grated zest of 1 orange as you butter and fold the layers, adding only a little zest at a time.

Each serving provides Ⓥ

kcal 280, **protein** 4 g, **fat** 16 g (of which saturated fat 4 g), **carbohydrate** 31 g (of which sugars 18 g), **fibre** 3 g

✓✓	E
✓	copper

good puddings

Strawberry cheese tart

Here a very thin, crisp pastry case is filled with a creamy orange-flavoured filling – a delicious light alternative to pastry cream – and covered with luscious strawberries and blueberries. A sweet glaze is the finishing touch.

Serves 6

Pastry case
115 g (4 oz) plain flour
55 g (2 oz) unsalted butter, at room
     temperature
2 tbsp caster sugar
2 egg yolks

Filling
225 g (8 oz) reduced-fat soft cheese
1 tbsp clear honey
grated zest of 1 orange
1 tbsp orange juice
225 g (8 oz) ripe strawberries, quartered
55 g (2 oz) blueberries
4 tbsp redcurrant jelly

Preparation time: 30 minutes, plus 1½ hours
     chilling and cooling to set
Cooking time: 15–20 minutes

Each serving provides   Ⓥ
kcal 260, **protein** 6 g, **fat** 10 g (of which
saturated fat 6 g), **carbohydrate** 39 g (of
which sugars 24 g), **fibre** 1 g

| ✓✓ | B$_{12}$, C |
| ✓ | A, B$_2$, E, calcium |

1 Sift the flour onto a cool work surface, make a well in the centre and put in the butter, sugar and egg yolks. Using the fingertips of one hand, work the ingredients in the centre together, then draw in the flour and work to a smooth paste. Put into a polythene bag and chill for 1 hour.

2 Roll out the pastry dough thinly on a floured surface and use to line a 21 cm (8½ in) loose-bottomed flan tin. Chill for 30 minutes.

3 Preheat the oven to 190°C (375°F, gas mark 5). Line the pastry case with greaseproof paper, fill with baking beans and bake 'blind' for 10–15 minutes or until lightly browned. Remove the paper and beans and bake for a further 5 minutes or until the base of the pastry case is cooked through. Allow to cool, then carefully remove the pastry case from the tin.

4 For the filling, mix together the soft cheese, honey and orange zest and juice until smooth. Spoon the filling into the pastry case and spread out evenly to the edges.

5 Arrange the strawberries and blueberries over the surface of the filling. Heat the redcurrant jelly until it is liquid and smooth, then brush generously over the fruit. Leave to cool and set before serving. The tart is best served within 1–2 hours of filling.

Some more ideas
● For a raspberry and peach tart, flavour the soft cheese with 1–2 tsp rosewater and 1 tbsp caster sugar instead of the honey and orange juice. Replace the strawberries and blueberries with 125 g (4½ oz) raspberries (or tayberries) and 3 ripe peaches, cut into neat slices. Glaze with melted apricot jam.

● For a mango and passion fruit tart, flavour the soft cheese with the sieved pulp of 2 passion fruit instead of the orange zest and juice. Replace the strawberries and blueberries with 1 large ripe mango, cut into neat slices, and glaze with melted apricot jam. Mango is a good source of vitamin A as beta-carotene, and the riper the fruit, the higher the vitamin A content. Antioxidant nutrients like beta-carotene and vitamin C protect the body against free radicals, and the need for these nutrients is further increased when people are exposed to environmental pollutants and smoking.

Plus points
● Strawberries and blueberries are rich sources of vitamin C.
● Reduced-fat soft cheese provides essential nutrients like protein and calcium with less fat and fewer calories.

good puddings

136

Black Forest mousse cake

This very light cake is almost fat-free, being based on egg whites whisked to firm peaks and folded together with flour, sugar and cocoa powder. Cocoa delivers a rich chocolate flavour without the fat of chocolate.

Serves 6

45 g (1½ oz) plain flour

5 tbsp cocoa powder

100 g (3½ oz) caster sugar

small pinch of salt

5 large egg whites

1 tsp pure vanilla extract

340 g (12 oz) sweet dark cherries, stoned
    and halved

1 tbsp icing sugar

To serve (optional)

3 tbsp fromage frais

1 tbsp cherry conserve

1–2 tbsp kirsch or rum (optional)

Preparation time: 15 minutes, plus cooling
Cooking time: 20–25 minutes

Each serving (cake alone) provides Ⓥ
kcal 180, **protein** 6 g, **fat** 3 g (of which
saturated fat 2 g), **carbohydrate** 34 g (of
which sugars 27 g), **fibre** 2 g

✓✓	copper
✓	iron

1 Preheat the oven to 180°C (350°F, gas mark 4). Line the bottom of a 23 cm (9 in) round deep cake tin with greaseproof paper.

2 Sift the flour, cocoa powder, half of the sugar and the salt into a bowl.

3 In another large bowl, which is perfectly clean and grease-free, whisk the egg whites until they are foamy. Continue whisking until they will hold a soft peak. Add the remaining sugar, 1 tbsp at a time, and the vanilla extract, while you continue to whisk the egg whites. Whisk until they are glossy and smooth, and will hold a firm peak.

4 Sprinkle the flour and cocoa mixture over the egg whites and fold in gently but thoroughly, taking care not to deflate the egg whites too much. Spoon the mixture into the tin. Smooth the surface gently. Sprinkle the cherries evenly over the top of the cake.

5 Bake for 20–25 minutes or until the cake has risen and is just firm to the touch yet still moist on top (a skewer inserted into the centre should come out clean). Remove from the oven and leave to cool.

6 Sprinkle the cake with the icing sugar before serving. If you want to serve with the fromage frais accompaniment, simply combine the fromage frais with the cherry conserve and optional kirsch or rum to taste.

Plus points

● Egg white still provides protein (9 g per 100 g/3½ oz), but has none of the fat or cholesterol found in egg yolk.

● Cocoa powder contains less fat than plain or milk chocolate, and five times as much iron. This iron is not as well absorbed as the iron in meat, but the vitamin C in the cherries will help the body to absorb it.

Some more ideas

● Canned stoned cherries in juice, drained, can be used if fresh cherries are not in season.

● Instead of cherries, use a combination of red soft fruits such as raspberries or small strawberries, or mixed fruit of the forest.

● For a vanilla cake, omit the cocoa powder and replace with the same amount of cornflour. To give an almond flavour instead of vanilla, use pure almond extract.

Sultana lemon cheesecake

Enjoy this thin but dense Italian-style cheesecake with its fresh lemon flavour with a cup of tea or as a dessert. Cheesecakes usually contain high levels of fat, but this recipe isn't baked with a butter-rich crust, and it uses lower-fat ricotta cheese rather than rich cream cheese, so the overall fat content is much reduced.

Serves 8

45 g (1½ oz) sultanas

3 tbsp brandy

3 tbsp semolina

340 g (12 oz) ricotta cheese

3 large egg yolks

85 g (3 oz) caster sugar

3 tbsp lemon juice

1½ tsp pure vanilla extract

finely grated zest of 2 large lemons

Topping

2 oranges

2 satsumas

1 lemon

4 tbsp lemon jelly marmalade

Preparation time: 20 minutes, plus 30 minutes soaking and 2–3 hours cooling

Cooking time: 35–40 minutes

Each serving provides ⓥ

kcal 220, **protein** 7 g, **fat** 7 g (of which saturated fat 4 g), **carbohydrate** 32 g (of which sugars 26 g), **fibre** 1 g

✓✓	C
✓	A, B$_{12}$, calcium

1 Place the sultanas in a small bowl, add the brandy and leave to soak for at least 30 minutes or until most of the brandy has been absorbed.

2 Preheat the oven to 180°C (350°F, gas mark 4). Line the bottom of a non-stick, 20 cm (8 in) loose-bottomed sandwich tin with buttered baking parchment. Lightly butter the side of the tin. Sprinkle 1 tbsp of the semolina into the tin, turn and tilt the tin to coat the bottom and sides, then tap out any excess semolina. Set the tin aside.

3 Put the ricotta cheese into a fine sieve and press it through into a mixing bowl. Beat in the egg yolks, sugar, lemon juice, vanilla extract and remaining semolina. Stir in the lemon zest and the sultanas with any remaining brandy.

4 Spoon the mixture into the prepared tin and smooth the surface. Bake for 35–40 minutes or until the top is browned and the sides are shrinking from the tin. Leave to cool in the switched-off oven for 2–3 hours with the door ajar.

5 For the topping, peel the oranges, satsumas and lemon, removing all the white pith, then cut out the segments from between the membranes. Warm the marmalade very gently in a small saucepan until it has melted.

6 Carefully remove the cooled cheesecake from the tin and set on a serving platter. Brush with a layer of the melted marmalade. Arrange the citrus segments on top and glaze with the rest of the marmalade. Leave to set before serving.

Some more ideas

● Replace the sultanas with finely chopped dried apricots or sour cherries.

● For a mixed citrus flavour, add grated lime and orange zests, and soak the sultanas in orange juice. Replace the lemon juice with orange juice.

● Alternative fruit toppings include halved strawberries, blueberries and raspberries.

Plus points

● Many cheesecake recipes include finely ground nuts to help to bind the ingredients together. In this recipe the nuts have been replaced by semolina, which is finely ground durum wheat, thus omitting the fat that nuts would have supplied.

● The fresh citrus fruit topping provides lots of vitamin C.

good puddings

Summer pudding

What an amazing dish the British summer pudding is – simplicity itself, and as perfect as a midsummer's day. The peaches or nectarines add a slightly different dimension to this version, a marvellous way of eating a nice large portion of ripe fresh fruit, not cooked at all so as to retain all its nutrients.

Serves 6

600 g (1 lb 5 oz) mixed summer fruit (raspberries, blueberries, redcurrants, sliced strawberries)

2 ripe peaches or nectarines, stoned and diced

3 tbsp sugar, or to taste

150 ml (5 fl oz) cranberry juice

8 thin slices white bread, about 200 g (7 oz) in total, preferably 1–2 days old

To serve (optional)

reduced-fat crème fraîche

Preparation time: 20 minutes, plus 2 hours macerating and 8 hours chilling

1 Crush the different types of fruit individually, to be sure all the skins are broken and the fruit is pulpy. Put all the fruit in a large bowl with the sugar and cranberry juice and stir to mix. Leave to macerate for 2 hours.

2 Cut the crusts from the bread and cut the slices into strips or triangles. Fit the bread into a 1 litre (2 pint) pudding basin to line the bottom and sides, reserving enough bread to cover the top. Fill in any gaps with small bits of bread.

3 Reserve 3–4 tbsp of juice from the mixed fruit, then gently pour the fruit mixture into the bread-lined pudding basin. Top with the remaining bread. Cover with a plate that just fits inside the rim of the basin, setting it directly on top of the bread, and then place a heavy weight such as a can of food on top. Place the basin in the fridge to chill for 8 hours or overnight.

4 To serve, turn the pudding out onto a serving dish. Use the reserved fruit juice to brush or pour over any parts of the bread that have not been coloured. Serve with crème fraîche, if liked.

Some more ideas

● Use an enriched bread such as Jewish challah or brioche instead of white bread.

● For an autumn pudding, substitute raisin bread for white bread, and instead of the summer fruits and peaches, use 2 large dessert apples, diced, 2 pears, diced, 30 g (1 oz) sultanas, 30 g (1 oz) dried cranberries and 50 g (1¾ oz) dried apricots, chopped. Put the fruit in a saucepan with 300 ml (10 fl oz) apple juice and ½ tsp ground cinnamon. Bring to the boil, then poach gently for 5–7 minutes or until the apples are tender. Pour into the bread-lined mould and weight as in step 3. Serve decorated with diced sharon fruit and/or a scattering of pomegranate seeds, if you like.

Plus points

● Raspberries, redcurrants and strawberries are an excellent source of vitamin C (blueberries are a good source). This vitamin is not only an antioxidant with an important role in preventing heart disease, but is also essential for good wound-healing and resistance to infections.

● Low in fat and high in carbohydrate and fibre, this is a delicious dessert in a diet for a healthy heart.

Each serving (pudding alone) provides Ⓥ

kcal 160, **protein** 4 g, **fat** 1 g, **carbohydrate** 36 g (of which sugars 20 g), **fibre** 3 g

✓✓✓ C

✓ folate, niacin

Apple crème caramel

Most traditional recipes for crème caramel are made with a sugar-based caramel and a rich creamy custard. The fruity version here uses apple juice both for the caramel and in the custard, thus reducing the fat and sugar content. Served with blackberries, or another seasonal fruit, this is a delicious treat for family or friends.

Serves 6
Caramel
750 ml (1¼ pints) clear apple juice
pinch of ground cinnamon
Custard
3 eggs
3 egg yolks
55 g (2 oz) sugar
600 ml (1 pint) clear apple juice
To serve
300 g (10½ oz) blackberries

Preparation time: 35 minutes, plus at least
    2 hours chilling
Cooking time: 35–40 minutes

Each serving provides ⓥ
kcal 210, **protein** 6 g, **fat** 6 g (of which
saturated fat 2 g), **carbohydrate** 34 g (of
which sugars 34 g), **fibre** 1 g

| ✓✓ | B$_{12}$, C, E |
| ✓ | A, potassium |

1 Preheat the oven to 160°C (325°F, gas mark 3).

2 To make the caramel, put the apple juice in a large, heavy, non-reactive saucepan with the cinnamon. Bring to the boil, then cook over a high heat for about 20 minutes or until reduced by about half. Lower the heat to moderate and continue boiling down for a further 10 minutes or until thickened to a bubbling darkish syrup. Take care, as it burns very easily at this stage.

3 Remove from the heat and pour into 6 ramekins (150 ml/5 fl oz capacity). Swirl the apple caramel round the sides if you can, or use a spoon and spread it around a bit. It will not swirl round as easily as ordinary caramel would, so do not worry.

4 For the custard, beat the eggs and egg yolks with the sugar until smooth. Heat the apple juice in a saucepan until it comes to the boil, then slowly stir it into the egg mixture, mixing well. Pour the custard into the 6 caramel-lined ramekins.

5 Set the ramekins in a roasting tin. Pour hot water into the tin to come about halfway up the sides of the ramekins. Bake for 35–40 minutes or until the custard has just set. Remove the ramekins from the tin. Leave to cool, then chill for at least 2 hours.

6 To serve, loosen each custard with a knife run round the edge, then turn out onto a plate where it will be surrounded by its own pool of apple caramel sauce. Serve with the fresh blackberries.

Plus points
● Apple juice provides good amounts of potassium, which is so important in getting the balance with sodium right for healthy blood pressure and a healthy heart.
● Blackberries are unusual among fruits in that they are a very rich source of vitamin E. Their vitamin C content is high too.

Another idea
● For Spanish orange custards (*Flans de naranjas*), which are a beautiful orange colour, omit the caramel and use 750 ml (1¼ pints) of orange juice instead of apple juice in the custard. Heat the orange juice with the zest of 1 orange, taken with a citrus zester or grated, and slowly beat into the egg and sugar mixture. Pour into 6 moulds and bake as above. Serve the orange custard with fresh orange slices – a mixture of ordinary and blood oranges would be stunning. The raw oranges are packed with vitamin C.

Raspberry frozen yogurt

This frozen yogurt, exotically flavoured with rosewater and crème de cassis, is much lower in sugar than bought frozen yogurt. Serve scoops on their own, or pile into sundae glasses with fresh fruit and sprigs of mint.

Serves 8

500 g (1 lb 2 oz) raspberries
4 tbsp seedless raspberry jam
2 tbsp rosewater
2 tbsp crème de cassis (optional)
500 g (1 lb 2 oz) Greek-style yogurt
3 tbsp icing sugar, or to taste

To decorate (optional)
raspberries
fresh mint leaves

Preparation time: 15–20 minutes, plus freezing
(varies according to method used)

Each serving provides Ⓥ

kcal 140, **protein** 5 g, **fat** 6 g (of which
saturated fat 3 g), **carbohydrate** 19 g (of
which sugars 19 g), **fibre** 2 g

✓✓ C

✓   folate, calcium

---

1 Put the raspberries into a saucepan and add the raspberry jam. Warm over a low heat for about 5 minutes or until the raspberries are pulpy, stirring occasionally.

2 Press the raspberries and their juice through a nylon sieve into a bowl; discard the pips in the sieve. Stir in the rosewater and the crème de cassis, if using. Whisk in the yogurt until smoothly blended. Taste the mixture and sweeten with the icing sugar.

3 Pour into an ice-cream machine and freeze according to the manufacturer's instructions. When you have a smooth and creamy frozen mixture, spoon it into a rigid freezerproof container. Freeze for at least 1 hour. If you do not have an ice-cream machine, pour the mixture straight into a large freezerproof container and freeze for 1 hour or until set round the edges. Beat until the mixture is smooth, then return to the freezer. Freeze for 30 minutes, then beat again. Repeat the freezing and beating several times more until the frozen yogurt has a smooth consistency, then leave it to freeze for at least 1 hour.

4 If storing in the freezer for longer than 1 hour, transfer the frozen yogurt to the fridge 20 minutes before serving, to soften slightly. Decorate with raspberries and mint, if liked.

Plus points

• Although Greek-style yogurt is regarded as extremely rich and creamy-tasting, it is surprising to find that it has just 17 kcal per level tbsp, while double cream has an amazing 67 kcal for the same amount.

• Raspberries are an excellent source of vitamin C, whether fresh or frozen. If freshly picked there may be more C, but it is not always easy to tell how long fruit has been sitting on the shelf, and vitamin C content will be going down steadily following picking. Frozen fruits are usually processed immediately after picking and may therefore be a richer source of this vital vitamin.

Some more ideas

• Use frozen raspberries instead of fresh.

• For a frozen yogurt flavoured with mango and orange-flower water, replace the raspberries and jam with 2 cans mangoes, 425 g each, drained and puréed, and use orange-flower water and Cointreau instead of the rosewater and cassis. There should be no need to sweeten the mixture. Mangoes are an excellent source of beta-carotene, which the body can convert into vitamin A.

good puddings

Tropical trifle

This trifle is bursting with exotic fruits – mango, banana, granadilla, papaya, lime and carambola, all supplying lots of flavour as well as essential vitamins. And the trifle looks as special as it tastes.

Serves 6

185 g (6½ oz) fatless sponge or Madeira cake, sliced

grated zest and juice of 1 lime

grated zest and juice of 1 orange

3 tbsp medium sherry or Madeira

1 small ripe mango

2 bananas

1 papaya

3 granadillas, halved

100 ml (3½ fl oz) whipping cream

1 tbsp clear honey

100 g (3½ oz) plain low-fat bio yogurt

Custard

2 egg yolks

2 tsp cornflour

2 tbsp caster sugar

300 ml (10 fl oz) semi-skimmed milk

To decorate

1 tbsp toasted desiccated coconut

2 carambola, sliced

Preparation time: 20 minutes, plus cooling

Each serving provides   Ⓥ

kcal 350, **protein** 7 g, **fat** 16 g (of which saturated fat 9 g), **carbohydrate** 47 g (of which sugars 34 g), **fibre** 2 g

✓✓✓	C
✓✓	A, B$_{12}$
✓	B$_2$, B$_6$, E, niacin, calcium, copper, potassium

1 Arrange the slices of cake to cover the bottom of a wide glass serving bowl. Mix together the lime and orange juices and sherry or Madeira, and sprinkle over the cake to moisten. Purée the mango flesh in a food processor or by pressing through a sieve, and spread over the cake slices. Set aside.

2 To make the custard, put the egg yolks, cornflour and sugar in a bowl and beat until smooth. Put the milk in a saucepan with the lime and orange zests and bring to the boil. Slowly pour onto the egg yolks, stirring thoroughly. Return the mixture to the pan and cook over a low heat, stirring constantly, until thickened to a custard consistency. Remove from the heat and leave to cool slightly.

3 Slice the bananas and papaya and arrange over the cake. Scoop the pulp from the granadillas and scatter over the top. Pour the custard evenly over the fruit and leave to cool completely and set.

4 Whip the cream until thick. Gently whip in the honey and yogurt, then spread the mixture over the top of the trifle. Sprinkle the surface with the toasted coconut and decorate with the slices of carambola.

Some more ideas

● Use passion fruit instead of granadillas, or omit the granadillas if you prefer a smooth-textured trifle.

● Replace the papaya with 170 g (6 oz) sliced strawberries. Omit the lime and use the zest and juice of 2 oranges. For moistening the cake, mix the orange juice with orange liqueur instead of sherry.

● Instead of mango, top the moistened cake with a fresh guava purée, made by puréeing 170 g (6 oz) chopped ripe guavas with 4–6 tsp sugar and then sieving. Alternatively, use fresh puréed apricots, omitting the sugar.

Plus points

● The bananas in this recipe are a useful source of potassium, which is important in preventing high blood pressure. There are plenty of other 'heart-healthy' vitamins and minerals here too, such as vitamin C in the citrus and papaya and vitamin A offered by the carambola.

● Mangoes are an excellent source of beta-carotene, which the body can convert to vitamin A. This vitamin is essential for healthy skin and good vision, especially in a dim light. Beta-carotene is also now recognised as a powerful antioxidant, valuable in the prevention of coronary heart disease and cancer.

Strawberry and cranberry granita

A granita is a refreshing alternative to ice-cream, with a delightful texture. Make this in strawberry season, when the berries are at their peak of sweet flavour and perfume – if your strawberries are very ripe and sweet, you won't need to add much sugar. The granita is served with a strawberry sauce.

Serves 4

500 g (1 lb 2 oz) ripe strawberries, sliced
85 g (3 oz) caster sugar, or to taste
240 ml (8 fl oz) cranberry juice
strawberries or mixed strawberries and
  raspberries to decorate

Preparation time: 15 minutes, plus 30 minutes
  macerating and about 2 hours freezing

1 Put the strawberries in a bowl, sprinkle over the sugar and toss together. Cover and leave to macerate at room temperature for 30 minutes.

2 Tip the strawberry mixture into a food processor or blender and process to a smooth purée. Taste the purée and add more sugar according to taste and the sweetness of the fruit. Reserve 150 ml (5 fl oz) of the purée to serve as a sauce.

3 Mix the remainder of the purée with the cranberry juice. Place in a shallow metal tray and freeze for about 30 minutes or until the mixture has set softly round the edge.

4 Using a fork, scrape the partially frozen mixture from the edge into the still liquid centre. Return the tray to the freezer and freeze for a further 20 minutes. Scrape the frozen edge into the centre again, then return to the freezer once more. Repeat the scraping and freezing two or three more times, until you have a mixture that consists of separate, almost fluffy, soft ice crystals.

5 Serve the granita in dessert goblets or in bowls, decorated with a few berries and accompanied with the sauce.

Some more ideas

● To increase the fruit content of this dessert even more, serve it layered with more berries or other sliced fruit.

● For a quick sorbet, freeze the mixture in an ice cube tray, with dividers, until firm, then pop the cubes out of the tray and whiz in a food processor with about 6 tbsp cranberry juice, or just enough to achieve a light and fluffy consistency. Serve straightaway.

● Make the mixture into a sorbet using an ice-cream machine, following the manufacturer's instructions.

● Add sliced ripe peaches to the berry garnish, to boost the vitamin C content.

Plus points

● Strawberries offer more vitamin C than any other berry (77 mg per 100 g/3½ oz, as compared with raspberries at 32 mg and blackberries at 15 mg). They are also low in calories – a portion of 100 g (3½ oz) contains just 27 kcal.

● Cranberry juice contains a compound that prevents *E.coli* bacteria from causing urinary-tract infections.

Each serving provides Ⓥ

kcal 140, protein 1 g, fat 0 g, carbohydrate 36 g (of which sugars 36 g), fibre 1 g

✓✓✓ C

good puddings

Persian almond-milk jelly

This irridescent milk jelly, delicately perfumed with almond, is set off to perfection by the exotic flavours and beautiful colours of the mixed fruit salad. Very little sugar is needed as the fruit provides natural sweetness.

Serves 4

500 ml (17 fl oz) semi-skimmed milk

2 tsp powdered gelatine

2 tbsp caster sugar

1 tsp pure almond extract

Fruit salad

3 oranges

3 tbsp caster sugar

2 cardamom pods, very lightly crushed

1 tbsp lemon juice

1 tbsp orange-flower water, or more to taste

2 bananas

½ pomegranate

Preparation time: 30 minutes, plus cooling and several hours chilling to set

Each serving provides

kcal 200, **protein** 8 g, **fat** 2 g (of which saturated fat 1 g), **carbohydrate** 39 g (of which sugars 38 g), **fibre** 3 g

✓✓✓	C
✓✓	calcium
✓	B$_{12}$, potassium

1 Pour 150 ml (5 fl oz) of the milk into a saucepan. Sprinkle over the gelatine and leave to sponge for 5 minutes without stirring.

2 Stir in the sugar and set the pan over a low heat. Cook gently, without boiling, until the sugar and gelatine have completely dissolved, stirring frequently. Remove from the heat and add the remaining milk and the almond extract. Stir to mix. Pour into four 175 ml (6 fl oz) decorative jelly moulds. Cover and chill for several hours or until set.

3 Meanwhile, peel the zest thinly from 1 orange and cut into thin strips. Squeeze the juice from the orange into a saucepan and add the zest, the sugar, cardamom pods and 150 ml (5 fl oz) of water. Heat gently, stirring, until the sugar dissolves, then bring to the boil. Boil for 5–10 minutes or until reduced and syrupy. Remove from the heat and stir in the lemon juice and orange-flower water. Leave to cool.

4 Peel the remaining 2 oranges, removing all the white pith, and cut across into slices. Peel and slice the bananas. Scoop out the seeds from the pomegranate half. Combine the fruit in a bowl and pour on the syrup.

5 Turn out the jellies onto individual plates. Surround with fruit salad and serve immediately.

Plus points

● Milk jellies were a popular dessert with the Victorians and a regular feature of nursery menus, because nannies recognised that the calcium provided by milk is particularly important for growing children to build strong bones.

Some more ideas

● For a banana-almond milk jelly, mash 3 ripe bananas, or purée with a hand-held blender. Mix with the milk, sugar and ½ tsp each pure vanilla extract and pure almond extract. Sponge 2 sachets powdered gelatine in 2 tbsp cold water. Heat the banana mixture almost to boiling, whisking or stirring constantly, then remove from the heat and stir in the gelatine until completely dissolved. Pour into a 900 ml (1½ pint) decorative mould and chill until set.

● For a berry and red wine jelly, use 360 ml (12 fl oz) cranberry juice and 150 ml (5 fl oz) fruity red wine. Purée 250 g (9 oz) mixed blackberries and blueberries, then press through a sieve to remove the pips. Mix the purée with the cranberry juice and wine. Use 2 tbsp caster sugar and 2 sachets powdered gelatine, sponging and dissolving it as above. If you like, add a good pinch of ground allspice to the mixture. Pour into a 900 ml (1½ pint) decorative mould and chill until set.

Sweet balsamic berry ice-cream

Capture the flavour of summer's bountiful fruit basket to enjoy later in the year with this luscious yet reduced-fat ice-cream. Made with a light sugar syrup rather than a thick egg custard, it has a fresh flavour that is highlighted with a splash of balsamic vinegar. The ice-cream is perfectly partnered with a berry compote.

Serves 6

450 g (1 lb) strawberries

250 g (9 oz) raspberries

200 g (7 oz) blueberries

2 tsp best-quality balsamic vinegar

200 g (7 oz) caster sugar

150 ml (5 fl oz) double cream, lightly
    whipped

sprigs of fresh mint to decorate

Strawberry compote

450 g (1 lb) strawberries

1–2 tsp caster sugar

balsamic vinegar

black pepper

Preparation time: about 20 minutes, plus
    cooling and at least 30 minutes chilling and
    freezing (varies according to method used)

Each serving provides

kcal 310, **protein** 2 g, **fat** 12 g (of which
saturated fat 7 g), **carbohydrate** 50 g (of
which sugars 50 g), **fibre** 3 g

| ✓✓✓ | C |
| ✓ | folate |

1 Place the strawberries, raspberries and blueberries in a food processor or blender and process until smooth. Press through a fine nylon sieve into a large measuring jug to remove the pips and blueberry skins. Stir in the balsamic vinegar, then chill for 30 minutes.

2 Meanwhile, place the sugar and 150 ml (5 fl oz) of water in a small saucepan over a high heat. Stir until the sugar dissolves. Bring to the boil, without stirring, and boil for 5 minutes until a light syrup forms. Pour into a heatproof bowl and leave to cool, then stir in the puréed berry mixture and leave to chill until required.

3 Add the whipped cream to the berry mixture in the bowl, and fold in. Pour into an ice-cream machine and freeze according to the manufacturer's instructions. Then transfer to a freezerproof container and freeze for at least 2 hours before serving. If you do not have an ice-cream machine, pour the mixture straight into a large freezerproof container and freeze for 1 hour or until set round the edges. Beat until the mixture is smooth, then return to the freezer. Freeze for 30 minutes, then beat again. Repeat the freezing and beating several times more until the ice-cream has a smooth consistency, then leave it to freeze for at least 2 hours.

4 To make the strawberry compote, slice the berries into a serving bowl. Sprinkle with sugar to taste, then add a splash of balsamic vinegar and a little freshly ground black pepper. Stir, then chill until ready to serve.

5 Transfer the ice-cream to the fridge 20 minutes before serving to allow it to soften. Scoop into individual bowls and top with the strawberry compote. Decorate with sprigs of mint and serve.

Some more ideas

● For a vibrant yellow tropical ice-cream, peel, stone and slice 2 ripe mangoes and 2 ripe peaches. Place in a food processor and purée, then follow the recipe as above, substituting 1 tbsp fresh lime juice for the balsamic vinegar. Serve with a selection of sliced fresh tropical fruit, including papaya, mango and kiwi fruit.

Plus points

● Strawberries, raspberries and blueberries combine to make this dessert an excellent source of vitamin C, which has a vital role to play in repairing damaged tissues and in wound healing. Vitamin C also helps to maintain the immune system and is a powerful antioxidant, helping to prevent degenerative disease.

good puddings

154

A glossary of nutritional terms

Antioxidants These are compounds that help to protect the body's cells against the damaging effects of free radicals. Vitamins C and E, beta-carotene (the plant form of vitamin A) and the mineral selenium, together with many of the phytochemicals found in fruit and vegetables, all act as antioxidants.

Calorie A unit used to measure the energy value of food and the intake and use of energy by the body. The scientific definition of 1 calorie is the amount of heat required to raise the temperature of 1 gram of water by 1 degree Centigrade. This is such a small amount that in this country we tend to use the term kilocalories (abbreviated to *kcal*), which is equivalent to 1000 calories. Energy values can also be measured in kilojoules (kJ): 1 kcal = 4.2 kJ.

A person's energy (calorie) requirement varies depending on his or her age, sex and level of activity. The estimated average daily energy requirements are:

Age (years)	Female (kcal)	Male (kcal)
1–3	1165	1230
4–6	1545	1715
7–10	1740	1970
11–14	1845	2220
15–18	2110	2755
19–49	1940	2550
50–59	1900	2550
60–64	1900	2380
65–74	1900	2330

Carbohydrates These energy-providing substances are present in varying amounts in different foods and are found in three main forms: sugars, starches and non-starch polysaccharides (NSP), usually called fibre.

There are two types of sugars: *intrinsic sugars*, which occur naturally in fruit (fructose) and sweet-tasting vegetables, and *extrinsic sugars*, which include lactose (from milk) and all the non-milk extrinsic sugars (NMEs) – sucrose (table sugar), honey, treacle, molasses and so on. The NMEs, or 'added' sugars, provide only calories, whereas foods containing intrinsic sugars also offer vitamins, minerals and fibre. Added sugars (*simple carbohydrates*) are digested and absorbed rapidly to provide energy very quickly. Starches and fibre (*complex carbohydrates*), on the other hand, break down more slowly to offer a longer-term energy source (see also Glycaemic Index). Starchy carbohydrates are found in bread, pasta, rice, wholegrain and breakfast cereals, and potatoes and other starchy vegetables such as parsnips, sweet potatoes and yams.

Healthy eating guidelines recommend that at least half of our daily energy (calories) should come from carbohydrates, and that most of this should be from complex carbohydrates. No more than 11% of our total calorie intake should come from 'added' sugars. For an average woman aged 19–49 years, this would mean a total carbohydrate intake of 259 g per day, of which 202 g should be from starch and intrinsic sugars and no more than 57 g from added sugars. For a man of the same age, total carbohydrates each day should be about 340 g (265 g from starch and intrinsic sugars and 75 g from added sugars).

See also Fibre and Glycogen.

Cholesterol There are two types of cholesterol – the soft waxy substance called blood cholesterol, which is an integral part of human cell membranes, and dietary cholesterol, which is contained in food. *Blood cholesterol* is important in the formation of some hormones and it aids digestion. High blood cholesterol levels are known to be an important risk factor for coronary heart disease, but most of the cholesterol in our blood is made by the liver – only about 25% comes from cholesterol in food. So while it would seem that the amount of cholesterol-rich foods in the diet would have a direct effect on blood cholesterol levels, in fact the best way to reduce blood cholesterol is to eat less saturated fat and to increase intake of foods containing soluble fibre.

Fat Although a small amount of fat is essential for good health, most people consume far too much. Healthy eating guidelines recommend that no more than 33% of our daily energy intake (calories) should come from fat. Each gram of fat contains 9 kcal, more than twice as many calories as carbohydrate or protein, so for a woman aged 19–49 years this means a daily maximum of 71 g fat, and for a man in the same age range 93.5 g fat.

Fats can be divided into 3 main groups: saturated, monounsaturated and polyunsaturated, depending on the chemical structure of the fatty acids they contain. *Saturated fatty acids* are found mainly in animal fats such as butter and other dairy products and in fatty meat. A high intake of saturated fat is known to be a risk factor for coronary heart disease and certain types of cancer. Current guidelines are that no more than 10% of our daily calories should come from saturated fats, which is about 21.5 g for an adult woman and 28.5 g for a man.

Where saturated fats tend to be solid at room temperature, the *unsaturated fatty acids* – monounsaturated and polyunsaturated – tend to be liquid. *Monounsaturated fats* are found predominantly in olive oil, groundnut (peanut) oil, rapeseed oil and avocados. Foods high in *polyunsaturates* include most vegetable oils – the exceptions are palm oil and coconut oil, both of which are saturated.

Both saturated and monounsaturated fatty acids can be made by the body, but certain polyunsaturated fatty acids – known as *essential fatty acids* – must be supplied by food. There are 2 'families' of these essential fatty acids: *omega-6*, derived from linoleic acid, and *omega-3*, from linolenic acid. The main food sources of the omega-6 family are vegetable oils such as olive and sunflower; omega-3 fatty acids are provided by oily fish, nuts, and vegetable oils such as soya and rapeseed.

When vegetable oils are hydrogenated (hardened) to make margarine and reduced-fat spreads, their unsaturated fatty acids can be changed into trans fatty acids, or '*trans fats*'. These artificially produced trans fats are believed to act in the same way as saturated fats within the body – with the same risks to health. Current healthy eating guidelines suggest that no more than 2% of our daily calories should come from trans fats, which is about 4.3 g for an adult woman and 5.6 g for a man. In thinking about the amount of trans fats you consume, remember that major sources are processed foods such as biscuits, pies, cakes and crisps.

Fibre Technically non-starch polysaccharides (NSP), fibre is the term commonly used to describe several different compounds, such as pectin, hemicellulose, lignin and gums, which are found in the cell walls of all plants. The body cannot digest fibre, nor does it have much nutritional value, but it plays an important role in helping us to stay healthy.

Fibre can be divided into 2 groups – soluble and insoluble. Both types are provided by most plant foods, but some foods are particularly good sources of one type or the other. *Soluble fibre* (in oats, pulses, fruit and vegetables) can help to reduce high blood cholesterol levels and to control blood sugar levels by slowing down the absorption of sugar. *Insoluble fibre* (in wholegrain cereals, pulses, fruit and vegetables) increases stool bulk and speeds the passage of waste material through the body. In this way it helps to prevent constipation, haemorrhoids and diverticular disease, and may protect against bowel cancer.

Our current intake of fibre is around 12 g a day. Healthy eating guidelines suggest that we need to increase this amount to 18 g a day.

Free radicals These highly reactive molecules can cause damage to cell walls and DNA (the genetic material found within cells). They are believed to be involved in the development of heart disease, some cancers and premature ageing. Free radicals are produced naturally by

glossary

the body in the course of everyday life, but certain factors, such as cigarette smoke, pollution and over-exposure to sunlight, can accelerate their production.

Gluten A protein found in wheat and, to a lesser degree, in rye, barley and oats, but not in corn (maize) or rice. People with *coeliac disease* have a sensitivity to gluten and need to eliminate all gluten-containing foods, such as bread, pasta, cakes and biscuits, from their diet.

Glycaemic Index (GI) This is used to measure the rate at which carbohydrate foods are digested and converted into sugar (glucose) to raise blood sugar levels and provide energy. Foods with a high GI are quickly broken down and offer an immediate energy fix, while those with a lower GI are absorbed more slowly, making you feel full for longer and helping to keep blood sugar levels constant. High-GI foods include table sugar, honey, mashed potatoes and watermelon. Low-GI foods include pulses, wholewheat cereals, apples, cherries, dried apricots, pasta and oats.

Glycogen This is one of the 2 forms in which energy from carbohydrates is made available for use by the body (the other is *glucose*). Whereas glucose is converted quickly from carbohydrates and made available in the blood for a fast energy fix, glycogen is stored in the liver and muscles to fuel longer-term energy needs. When the body has used up its immediate supply of glucose, the stored glycogen is broken down into glucose to continue supplying energy.

Minerals These inorganic substances perform a wide range of vital functions in the body. The *macrominerals* – calcium, chloride, magnesium, potassium, phosphorus and sodium – are needed in relatively large quantities, whereas much smaller amounts are required of the remainder, called *microminerals*. Some microminerals (selenium, magnesium and iodine, for example) are needed in such tiny amounts that they are known as *'trace elements'*.

There are important differences in the body's ability to absorb minerals from different foods, and this can be affected by the presence of other substances. For example, oxalic acid, present in spinach, interferes with the absorption of much of the iron and calcium spinach contains.
- *Calcium* is essential for the development of strong bones and teeth. It also plays an important role in blood clotting. Good sources include dairy products, canned fish (eaten with their bones) and dark green, leafy vegetables.
- *Chloride* helps to maintain the body's fluid balance. The main source in the diet is table salt.
- *Chromium* is important in the regulation of blood sugar levels, as well as levels of fat and cholesterol in the blood. Good dietary sources include red meat, liver, eggs, seafood, cheese and wholegrain cereals.

- *Copper*, component of many enzymes, is needed for bone growth and the formation of connective tissue. It helps the body to absorb iron from food. Good sources include offal, shellfish, mushrooms, cocoa, nuts and seeds.
- *Iodine* is an important component of the thyroid hormones, which govern the rate and efficiency at which food is converted into energy. Good sources include seafood, seaweed and vegetables (depending on the iodine content of the soil in which they are grown).
- *Iron* is an essential component of haemoglobin, the pigment in red blood cells that carries oxygen around the body. Good sources are offal, red meat, dried apricots and prunes, and iron-fortified breakfast cereals.
- *Magnesium* is important for healthy bones, the release of energy from food, and nerve and muscle function. Good sources include wholegrain cereals, peas and other green vegetables, pulses, dried fruit and nuts.
- *Manganese* is a vital component of several enzymes that are involved in energy production and many other functions. Good dietary sources include nuts, cereals, brown rice, pulses and wholemeal bread.
- *Molybdenum* is an essential component of several enzymes, including those involved in the production of DNA. Good sources are offal, yeast, pulses, wholegrain cereals and green leafy vegetables.
- *Phosphorus* is important for healthy bones and teeth and for the release of energy from foods. It is found in most foods. Particularly good sources include dairy products, red meat, poultry, fish and eggs.
- *Potassium*, along with sodium, is important in maintaining fluid balance and regulating blood pressure, and is essential for the transmission of nerve impulses. Good sources include fruit, especially bananas and citrus fruits, nuts, seeds, potatoes and pulses.
- *Selenium* is a powerful antioxidant that protects cells against damage by free radicals. Good dietary sources are meat, fish, dairy foods, brazil nuts, avocados and lentils.
- *Sodium* works with potassium to regulate fluid balance, and is essential for nerve and muscle function. Only a little sodium is needed – we tend to get too much in our diet. The main source in the diet is table salt, as well as salty processed foods and ready-prepared foods.
- *Sulphur* is a component of 2 essential amino acids. Protein foods are the main source.
- *Zinc* is vital for normal growth, as well as reproduction and immunity. Good dietary sources include oysters, red meat, peanuts and sunflower seeds.

Phytochemicals These biologically active compounds, found in most plant foods, are believed to be beneficial in disease prevention. There are literally thousands of different phytochemicals, amongst which are the following:

- *Allicin*, a phytochemical found in garlic, onions, leeks, chives and shallots, is believed to help lower high blood cholesterol levels and stimulate the immune system.
- *Bioflavonoids*, of which there are at least 6000, are found mainly in fruit and sweet-tasting vegetables. Different bioflavonoids have different roles – some are antioxidants, while others act as anti-disease agents. A sub-group of these phytochemicals, called *flavonols*, includes the antioxidant *quercetin*, which is believed to reduce the risk of heart disease and help to protect against cataracts. Quercetin is found in tea, red wine, grapes and broad beans.
- *Carotenoids*, the best known of which are *beta-carotene* and *lycopene*, are powerful antioxidants thought to help protect us against certain types of cancer. Highly coloured fruits and vegetables, such as blackcurrants, mangoes, tomatoes, carrots, sweet potatoes, pumpkin and dark green, leafy vegetables, are excellent sources of carotenoids.
- *Coumarins* are believed to help protect against cancer by inhibiting the formation of tumours. Oranges are a rich source.
- *Glucosinolates*, found mainly in cruciferous vegetables, particularly broccoli, Brussels sprouts, cabbage, kale and cauliflower, are believed to have strong anti-cancer effects. *Sulphoraphane* is one of the powerful cancer-fighting substances produced by glucosinolates.
- *Phytoestrogens* have a chemical structure similar to the female hormone oestrogen, and they are believed to help protect against hormone-related cancers such as breast and prostate cancer. One of the types of these phytochemicals, called *isoflavones*, may also help to relieve symptoms associated with the menopause. Soya beans and chickpeas are a particularly rich source of isoflavones.

Protein This nutrient, necessary for growth and development, for maintenance and repair of cells, and for the production of enzymes, antibodies and hormones, is essential to keep the body working efficiently. Protein is made up of *amino acids*, which are compounds containing the 4 elements that are necessary for life: carbon, hydrogen, oxygen and nitrogen. We need all of the 20 amino acids commonly found in plant and animal proteins. The human body can make 12 of these, but the remaining 8 – called *essential amino acids* – must be obtained from the food we eat.

Protein comes in a wide variety of foods. Meat, fish, dairy products, eggs and soya beans contain all of the essential amino acids, and are therefore called first-class protein foods. Pulses, nuts, seeds and cereals are also good sources of protein, but do not contain the full range of essential amino acids. In practical terms, this really doesn't matter – as long as you include a variety of different protein foods in your diet, your body will get all the amino acids it needs. It is important, though, to eat protein foods every day because the essential amino acids cannot be stored in the body for later use.

The RNI of protein for women aged 19–49 years is 45 g per day and for men of the same age 55 g. In the UK most people eat more protein than they need, although this isn't normally a problem.

Reference Nutrient Intake (RNI) This denotes the average daily amount of vitamins and minerals thought to be sufficient to meet the nutritional needs of almost all individuals within the population. The figures, published by the Department of Health, vary depending on age, sex and specific nutritional needs such as pregnancy. RNIs are equivalent to what used to be called Recommended Daily Amounts or Allowances (RDA).

RNIs for adults (19–49 years)

Vitamin A	600–700 mcg
Vitamin B_1	0.8 mg for women, 1 mg for men
Vitamin B_2	1.1 mg for women, 1.3 mg for men
Niacin	13 mg for women, 17 mg for men
Vitamin B_6	1.2 mg for women, 1.4 mg for men
Vitamin B_{12}	1.5 mg
Folate	200 mcg (400 mcg for first trimester of pregnancy)
Vitamin C	40 mg
Vitamin E	no recommendation in the UK; the EC RDA is 10 mg, which has been used in all recipe analyses in this book
Calcium	700 mg
Chloride	2500 mg
Copper	1.2 mg
Iodine	140 mcg
Iron	14.8 mg for women, 8.7 mg for men
Magnesium	270–300 mg
Phosphorus	550 mg
Potassium	3500 mg
Selenium	60 mcg for women, 75 mcg for men
Sodium	1600 mg
Zinc	7 mg for women, 9.5 mg for men

Vitamins These are organic compounds that are essential for good health. Although they are required in only small amounts, each one has specific vital functions to perform. Most vitamins cannot be made by the human body, and therefore must be obtained from the diet. The body is capable of storing some vitamins (A, D, E, K and B_{12}), but the rest need to be provided by the diet on a regular basis. A well-balanced diet, containing a wide variety of different foods, is the best way to ensure that you get all the vitamins you need.

Vitamins can be divided into 2 groups: *water-soluble* (B complex and C) and *fat-soluble* (A, D, E and K). Water-soluble vitamins are easily destroyed during processing, storage, and the preparation and cooking of food. The fat-soluble vitamins are less vulnerable to losses during cooking and processing.

• *Vitamin A* (retinol) is essential for healthy vision, eyes, skin and growth. Good sources include dairy products, offal (especially liver), eggs and oily fish. Vitamin A can also be obtained from *beta-carotene*, the pigment found in highly coloured fruit and vegetables. In addition to acting as a source of vitamin A, beta-carotene has an important role to play as an antioxidant in its own right.

• *The B Complex vitamins* have very similar roles to play in nutrition, and many of them occur together in the same foods.

Vitamin B_1 (thiamin) is essential in the release of energy from carbohydrates. Good sources include milk, offal, meat (especially pork), wholegrain and fortified breakfast cereals, nuts and pulses, yeast extract and wheat germ. White flour and bread are fortified with B_1 in the UK.

Vitamin B_2 (riboflavin) is vital for growth, healthy skin and eyes, and the release of energy from food. Good sources include milk, meat, offal, eggs, cheese, fortified breakfast cereals, yeast extract and green leafy vegetables.

Niacin (nicotinic acid), sometimes called vitamin B_3, plays an important role in the release of energy within the cells. Unlike the other B vitamins it can be made by the body from the essential amino acid tryptophan. Good sources include meat, offal, fish, fortified breakfast cereals and pulses. White flour and bread are fortified with niacin in the UK.

Pantothenic acid, sometimes called vitamin B_5, is involved in a number of metabolic reactions, including energy production. This vitamin is present in most foods; notable exceptions are fat, oil and sugar. Good sources include liver, kidneys, yeast, egg yolks, fish roe, wheat germ, nuts, pulses and fresh vegetables.

Vitamin B_6 (pyridoxine) helps the body to utilise protein and contributes to the formation of haemoglobin for red blood cells. B_6 is found in a wide range of foods including meat, liver, fish, eggs, wholegrain cereals, some vegetables, pulses, brown rice, nuts and yeast extract.

Vitamin B_{12} (cyanocobalamin) is vital for growth, the formation of red blood cells and maintenance of a healthy nervous system. B_{12} is unique in that it is only found in foods of animal origin. Vegetarians who eat dairy products will get enough, but vegans need to ensure they include food fortified with B_{12} in their diet. Good sources of B_{12} include liver, kidneys, oily fish, meat, cheese, eggs and milk.

Folate (folic acid) is involved in the manufacture of amino acids and in the production of red blood cells. Recent research suggests that folate may also help to protect against heart disease. Good sources of folate are green leafy vegetables, liver, pulses, eggs, wholegrain cereal products and fortified breakfast cereals, brewers' yeast, wheatgerm, nuts and fruit, especially grapefruit and oranges.

Biotin is needed for various metabolic reactions and the release of energy from foods. Good sources include liver, oily fish, brewers' yeast, kidneys, egg yolks and brown rice.

• *Vitamin C* (ascorbic acid) is essential for growth and vital for the formation of collagen (a protein needed for healthy bones, teeth, gums, blood capillaries and all connective tissue). It plays an important role in the healing of wounds and fractures, and acts as a powerful antioxidant. Vitamin C is found mainly in fruit and vegetables.

• *Vitamin D* (cholecalciferol) is essential for growth and the absorption of calcium, and thus for the formation of healthy bones. It is also involved in maintaining a healthy nervous system. The amount of vitamin D occurring naturally in foods is small, and it is found in very few foods – good sources are oily fish (and fish liver oil supplements), eggs and liver, as well as breakfast cereals, margarine and full-fat milk that are fortified with vitamin D. Most vitamin D, however, does not come from the diet but is made by the body when the skin is exposed to sunlight.

• *Vitamin E* is not one vitamin, but a number of related compounds called tocopherols that function as antioxidants. Good sources of vitamin E are vegetable oils, polyunsaturated margarines, wheatgerm, sunflower seeds, nuts, oily fish, eggs, wholegrain cereals, avocados and spinach.

• *Vitamin K* is essential for the production of several proteins, including prothombin which is involved in the clotting of blood. It has been found to exist in 3 forms, one of which is obtained from food while the other 2 are made by the bacteria in the intestine. Vitamin K_1, which is the form found in food, is present in broccoli, cabbage, spinach, milk, margarine, vegetable oils, particularly soya oil, cereals, liver, alfalfa and kelp.

Nutritional analyses

The nutritional analysis of each recipe has been carried out using data from *The Composition of Foods* with additional data from food manufacturers where appropriate. Because the level and availability of different nutrients can vary, depending on factors like growing conditions and breed of animal, the figures are intended as an approximate guide only.

The analyses include vitamins A, B_1, B_2, B_6, B_{12}, niacin, folate, C, D and E, and the minerals calcium, copper, iron, potassium, selenium and zinc. Other vitamins and minerals are not included as deficiencies are rare. Optional ingredients and optional serving suggestions have not been included in the calculations.

glossary

Index

Printing and binding: Printer Industria Gráfica
    S.A., Barcelona
Separations: Litho Origination, London
Paper: Perigord-Condat, France

index